PARNELL

PARNELL

A Play in Three Acts

BY

ELSIE T. SCHAUFFLER

SAMUEL FRENCH

NEW YORK   LOS ANGELES

SAMUEL FRENCH Ltd.   LONDON

1936

MANUFACTURED IN THE UNITED STATES OF AMERICA
BY THE VAIL-BALLOU PRESS, INC., BINGHAMTON, N. Y.

"PARNELL" was first produced by Robinson Smith and Frederick W. Ayer at the Ethel Barrymore Theatre in New York City on November 11, 1935. The play was staged by Guthrie McClintic, the settings and costumes were designed by Stewart Chaney, and the cast was as follows:

Played by

KATHARINE O'SHEA	*Margaret Rawlings*
MRS. BENJAMIN WOOD	*Effie Shannon*
PHYLLIS	*Ruth Yorke*
MRS. STEELE	*Ruth Matteson*
CLARA WOOD	*Phyllis Connard*
CAPTAIN WILLIAM HENRY O'SHEA	*John Emery*
THE O'GORMAN MAHON	*Gordon Burby*
TIMOTHY HEALY	*Joseph Holland*
THOMAS MURPHY	*Barry Macollum*
MICHAEL DAVITT	*Edward McNamara*
MONTAGU HARRISON	*Walter Holbrook*
PARNELL	*George Curzon*
GLADSTONE	*Alexander Frank*
MR. STANLEY	*Harry Redding*
JOHN REDMOND	*Clement O'Loghlen*
1st LEADER	*Barry Kelly*
2nd LEADER	*Charles Trexler*
3rd LEADER	*Winston O'Keefe*

TIME—England 1880–1890

ACT I

Scene 1—Katharine O'Shea's drawing room at Eltham, nine miles from London, April, 1880.

Scene 2—Committee Room 15, House of Commons—a few weeks later.

Scene 3—The drawing room at Eltham, the following Wednesday.

ACT II

Scene 1—The drawing room at Eltham, several years later.

Scene 2—The same, a month later.

ACT III

Scene 1—Gladstone's study, 10 Downing Street, late afternoon, autumn.

Scene 2—Committee Room 15, that evening.

Scene 3—The drawing room at Eltham, that night.

ACT ONE

ACT ONE

SCENE I

SCENE—KATHARINE O'SHEA'S *drawing room at Eltham, nine miles from London, May 1880. Late afternoon.*
It is a charming room, for in spite of the occasional fussiness of the period it is Georgian in mood. At the back are windows opening on the terrace. A door Left opens into the hall, piano above, and Right is a fireplace. MRS. BENJAMIN WOOD, "AUNT BEN" *is seated, her gold-headed, rubber-tipped cane by her side.*
KATHARINE O'SHEA *is standing, a newspaper in her hands from which she has been reading aloud. She is extraordinarily graceful. Her face sensitive, vivid, passionate.*
*As Curtain Rises—*KATIE *puts down one part of paper and starts on next section.*

KATIE. [*Reading.*] "The two successful candidates elected to represent County Clare were The O'Gorman Mahon and Captain William Henry O'Shea." [*Looking up from the paper.*] There is no mistake. It's true.

AUNT BEN. I never doubted it.

3

KATIE. *Willie* a member of Parliament. Aunt Ben, he'll want a bigger allowance.

AUNT BEN. [*Drily.*] Undoubtedly.

KATIE. That's probably why he is coming down here this afternoon. [*Throws down paper on piano stool.*] As a member of Parliament he will have new ways to spend money.

AUNT BEN. At any rate politics will at least keep him busy.

KATIE. I hope so.

AUNT BEN. Don't let it disturb you too much.

KATIE. I'll try.

AUNT BEN. You mustn't. You're much too young and much too pretty. Have you forgotten "The beautiful and young Mrs. O'Shea?"

KATIE. Oh, Aunt Ben, don't.

AUNT BEN. You are disturbed. What about?

KATIE. [*Crosses down to Right Center chair.*] Oh, nothing. I'm tired, I think.

AUNT BEN. Of what?

KATIE. Getting up, going to bed, dressing, undressing—hearing the clock tick. Aunt Ben, why does anyone marry anyone?

AUNT BEN. You probably married Willie for his yellow curls.

KATIE. Probably. But why should I be able to marry him —want to marry—live with him and then suddenly find him so repellent when he comes near me—even touches me?

AUNT BEN. I don't know, my dear. [KATIE *rises and crosses to Upper Right window.*] Katie, are you in love?

KATIE. No, I wish I were.

AUNT BEN. Heaven forbid. What is the matter with you then?

KATIE. —restless— Life's blowing by outside. It doesn't even touch me. My hair is not even ruffled.

AUNT BEN. That wind blows dust and dirt, Katie.

KATIE. And the smell of earth and trees—and sea. Oh, I'm ungrateful, Aunt Ben. The room is beautiful— but— [*With a smile.*] just a little stuffy. [*With a change of tone—backs down—picks up papers on floor.*] Well—Willie arrives by the five-two and I've decided something.

AUNT BEN. What?

KATIE. [*Crosses up to piano and places papers there.*] I simply won't give him any more of your money.

AUNT BEN. You'll have to give him something.

KATIE. I won't.

AUNT BEN. My dear, he isn't coming for a cup of tea. Money is easier than—other things.

KATIE. [*Crosses down.*] The holy bonds of matrimony. Ridiculous, isn't it? "These twain." Some day I shall kick over the traces.

AUNT BEN. You can't, Katie.

KATIE. Why not?

AUNT BEN. Because you were born Katharine Wood.

KATIE. I wish I had been born Katie Jones.

AUNT BEN. Well, you weren't, and it's only in the Bible people are born again. Somebody doubted it then. [KATIE *sits Left Center chair.*] Besides, my dear, what could you do? You can't divorce Willie. Of course he has provided you with grounds for divorce, about the only thing he has provided, but the law demands more than adultery. Personal violence added there-on-to.

KATIE. He hasn't knocked me down yet. I wish he would.

AUNT BEN. Yes—if you had witnesses. Remember, the law is on his side. You'll have to let him come here occasionally—

KATIE. I don't mind his coming if—

AUNT BEN. If he stays out of your bed. Well—he does, doesn't he?

KATIE. Yes.

AUNT BEN. Be tactful. All we have is money. Useful—but not always successful.

KATIE. I suppose that means liberal.

AUNT BEN. Oh, no, you can screw down the sum *total* if you like.

KATIE. If I *can*.

[*Enter* PHYLLIS, *a pretty Irish parlor-maid.*]

PHYLLIS. Excuse me, Ma'am. But your sister, Mrs. Steele, is calling. I've put her in the morning room, thinkin' you might be engaged.

KATIE. [*Looking at* AUNT BEN.] Annie!

AUNT BEN. [*No smile.*] We are honored.

KATIE. Show Mrs. Steele in, Phyllis.

PHYLLIS. Yes, Ma'am. [*She goes out.*]

AUNT BEN. When Annie leaves London a beautiful afternoon in the midst of the season—she must be fonder of us than I thought, Katie.

PHYLLIS. [*At the door.*] Mrs. Steele, Ma'am.

KATIE. [*Standing at Left Center chair.*] Annie, how nice of you.

ANNIE. [*Crossing to* KATIE—*kisses her on both cheeks.*] I'm fortunate to find you at home. [*To* AUNT BEN—*kisses and sits Right side of her.*] How do you do, Aunt Ben? How are you?

AUNT BEN. Fairly well, for an old woman deprived of all the things she likes to eat.

ANNIE. [*Solicitously.*] Another twinge of gout?

AUNT BEN. Annie, when you have gout, as you *undoubt-edly* will, you will not allude to it as a "twinge."

ANNIE. *So* sorry, dear.

AUNT BEN. How's Herbert?

ANNIE. Like all husbands—stodgy and busy.

ANNIE. [*To* AUNT BEN.] Where's Clara? Don't tell me she's visiting the poor such an afternoon as this.

AUNT BEN. Your sister Clara is sleeping. How Clara can sleep. Her conscience must be as a limpid pool. I should like to throw in a pebble and watch the ripples.

ANNIE. Perhaps the maiden star is conducive to a clear conscience.

AUNT BEN. Unlike the married then.

ANNIE. Isn't this news about Willie perfectly marvellous? Such fun for him. Seems incredible, though.

AUNT BEN. Ridiculous, but not incredible. How did you hear it, Annie?

ANNIE. [*Hesitates just the fraction of a second.*] Why— [*She notices the newspapers.*] Why, it's in the papers, isn't it? General election?

AUNT BEN. You so seldom read anything, Annie.

KATIE. Yes, it's in the papers and I've had a note from Willie. He's coming down this afternoon.

ANNIE. How pleased you must be. Since Willie sold his

commission in the Huzzars he really hasn't known what to do.

AUNT BEN. "Satan finds mischief" etc., etc.

ANNIE. Fancy Willie being addressed as the Honorable Member. Too amusing. He's so boyish looking. And fancy his running into the old O'Gorman Mahon!

AUNT BEN. Was that in the paper, too? [ANNIE *hesitates more obviously this time.* KATIE *who sees that* AUNT BEN *is baiting her, breaks in, smiling.*]

KATIE. Aunt Ben, I read it to you.

AUNT BEN. [*With a look at* KATIE *acknowledging the checkmate.*] So you did, my dear.

KATIE. The O'Gorman was an old beau of Aunt Ben's.

AUNT BEN. One of them.

ANNIE. Too thrilling.

AUNT BEN. Too conceited. I never did like handsome men. Preferred having the looks myself.

CLARA. [*Calling from outside the French window.*] Where are you, Katie?

AUNT BEN. [*Annoyed.*] Clara—I do wish she wouldn't follow me about.

KATIE. She's probably come to walk home with you.

CLARA. [*Outside.*] Oh, Katie—where are you?

KATIE. Let me tell her you're staying for dinner?

AUNT BEN. No—either her feelings would be hurt—or she would stay too.

CLARA. Katie—

KATIE. [*Rises—at the window.*] Here we are, Clara.

CLARA. [*Entering by the window. Crosses Center. Injured.*] You said you'd be in the garden this afternoon. Aunt Ben, I didn't know what had become of you. You told Morton you'd be home for tea.

AUNT BEN. Changed my mind.

CLARA. Morton became uneasy, so I told her I would walk over for you.

AUNT BEN. You and Morton must have very little to do.

CLARA. I'm sure I was only trying to be kind.

AUNT BEN. Well, you have been. I'm a cross old woman, so don't mind me. Here's Annie.

CLARA. [*Crosses Left and sits Left Center chair.*] Oh, Annie, I didn't see you. Have you just come?

ANNIE. Yes. Drove down. How are you, Clara?

CLARA. Can't complain.

PHYLLIS. [*At door.*] Excuse me, Ma'am. Will ye be after havin' it in the garden or here, Ma'am?

KATIE. Aunt Ben, what about the garden? Too cool?

CLARA. Very imprudent, Aunt Ben. The ground is damp.

AUNT BEN. The sunshine isn't.

KATIE. [*To* PHYLLIS.] In the garden. Take out plenty of rugs.

PHYLLIS. Yes, Ma'am. [*She goes.*]

[KATIE *crosses and sits in Right Center chair.*]

AUNT BEN. Katie has the loveliest garden this year. She's worked like a slave. What have you been doing with yourself, Annie?

ANNIE. Oh, the usual thing. London is a frightful crush this season. Saw Irving and Terry in Hamlet the other night.

KATIE. Oh, I must go up and see them.

ANNIE. I like something funnier, myself.

AUNT BEN. It shouldn't be hard to find something funnier than Hamlet.

ANNIE. Of course, Irving is wonderful.

AUNT BEN. Can't compare with Macready. [*Rises and takes her stick.*]

KATIE. I love Ellen Terry.

AUNT BEN. [*Moving toward the window en route to the garden for tea.*] Too "weepy."

KATIE. Aunt Ben! No! She walks in beauty.

[ANNIE *and* CLARA *rise.*]

AUNT BEN. [*Rises.*] Come pour my tea, Katie. Then

you can finish admiring Miss Terry. [AUNT BEN *exits with* CLARA.]

[KATIE *rises.* ANNIE *follows up as does* KATIE.]

ANNIE. [*As she moves toward the window pauses before a bowl of white roses.*] What lovely white roses, Katie!

KATIE. [*Picking the bowl up and bending her face over it.*] Aren't they! It's an Irish rose. Lady Londerry's gardener told her they couldn't be grown out of Ireland but I've done it. I sent her a box this morning.

ANNIE. [*Moving to the window.*] I should go in for flowers if I weren't so busy. Simply haven't the time.

KATIE. [*Without irony.*] I have so much.

ANNIE. My dear, it's ridiculous at your age shutting yourself up in the country. I can't think why you do it— We must arrange a party—you and Willie—

KATIE. [*Crosses to exit.*] Oh, no.

ANNIE. [*Talking steadily, goes through the window with* KATIE.] Why not? We'll dine and go to the play. Irving and Terry if you like. You're much too young— [*The voices die away. After a pause* PHYLLIS *shows in* CAPTAIN O'SHEA *and* THE O'GORMAN MAHON. O'SHEA, *blue-eyed and curly light hair, is foppish and overdressed, or at least too well-dressed for perfection and has an exaggerated English accent.* THE O'GORMAN *is a tall silver-haired old soldier of fortune. His mane is long and he has a roving eye for the ladies. His manner is reminiscent of the days of Louis Philippe.*]

O'SHEA. [*On entering.*] Tell your mistress, Captain O'Shea.

[PHYLLIS *starts for window.*]

O'GORMAN. Why not The O'Gorman Mahon and Captain O'Shea. It's proud she'll be to hear the name O'Gorman Mahon.

O'SHEA. The O'Gorman Mahon and Captain O'Shea.

PHYLLIS. [*Starts to harden.*] Yes, sir.

O'SHEA. Is your mistress alone?

PHYLLIS. [*Stops at Center of garden window.*] Mrs. O'Shea is in the garden with Mrs. Wood, Miss Wood and Mrs. Steele. [*Exits Upper Right.*]

O'GORMAN. Pretty wench. Is it a harem ye've got, Willie? And you concealin' it from me.

O'SHEA. [*Crosses to Left Center chair and sits. Somewhat annoyed at this pleasantry before a servant.*] My wife's aunt and sisters.

O'GORMAN. [THE O'GORMAN *on the contrary is completely at ease.*] And it's a cosy little place ye have here, Willie, nice, very nice indeed.

O'SHEA. Not my place—my wife's.

O'GORMAN. [*Sentimentally.*] Ah, happy wife. A beautiful home and a brave and handsome husband.

O'SHEA. She may like the happy home but the brave and handsome husband—that's another story.

O'GORMAN. You were always the modest one, Captain.
I'll warrant Mrs. O'Shea would tell me differently.

O'SHEA Your faith is touching, General, but please believe me, this isn't going to be any too easy.

O'GORMAN. Ah, Willie, what woman that ever lived
could resist you and me together. Have ye so soon for-
got the girls of County Clare.

O'SHEA. [*Humorously.*] My wife is not exactly that
type.

PHYLLIS. [*Crosses Upper Right Center.*] Mrs. O'Shea
will be here directly, Sir. Will ye be makin' yourselves
comfortable.

O'GORMAN. And what with, me dear?

O'SHEA. [*Rises. To* PHYLLIS.] Fetch whisky and soda.

PHYLLIS. Yes, Sir. [*She goes out.*]

O'GORMAN. Willie, Willie, why did ye stop me? Another
minute an' I'd a kissed her.

O'SHEA. [*Crossing to him.*] So I inferred. Look here,
General, we want to get on the good side of my wife. Do
you think flirting with her parlor-maid the best method?

O'GORMAN. Ye're right, me boy. Ye're right.

[PHYLLIS *enters with tray, decanter, syphon of soda
and glasses and places tray on table Down Right.*]

PHYLLIS. Will that be all, Sir?

O'SHEA. Thank you, yes.

[PHYLLIS *goes out.*]

O'GORMAN. [*Crosses to drinks Down Right. Then with a magnificent gesture, as though the house were his.*] Have a drink, me boy.

O'SHEA. Not now, thanks.

[KATIE *enters Upper Right.*]

KATIE. [*Coming in through the window.*] How do you do, Willie?

O'SHEA. [*Crosses up to her.*] Nice of you to be home. Katie, this is my colleague from County Clare, General The O'Gorman Mahon. General, my wife.

O'GORMAN. [*Bowing with much flourish.*] This is more happiness than I dared dream of. Madam, I now understand why Captain O'Shea was ever lonely.

KATIE. [*Smiling.*] Was he? Really?

O'GORMAN. [*Warming to the table.*] He was that lonely—

KATIE. But Willie is so brave. Once, when he was in Spain, he was lonely for eighteen months and only wrote me twice to mention it.

O'SHEA. There was nothing to write about.

KATIE. I know, and the Spanish mails are so uncertain. I won't tease you, Willie. Shame to me. Won't you sit down? Did you have a nice time in Ireland?

O'GORMAN. We kissed every pretty girl and drank with all the men.

O'SHEA. Ugh!

KATIE. [*Sits Right Center chair. With a laugh.*] Willie
loves Irish whisky so.

O'SHEA. Makes me ill to mention it.

O'GORMAN. But he drank it for the good of the State—
and the old County rewarded him. It's proud and glad
ye are, Ma'am, I'll warrant.

KATIE. Yes. Very glad.

O'GORMAN. What did I tell ye, Willie?

O'SHEA. Are you? Really, Katie?

KATIE. Yes—I'm glad—if you're interested. How did
you manage it? To get elected, I mean?

O'GORMAN. Through me. I hold County Clare like that—
[*Raises a clenched right hand.*] It was through me.

KATIE. How nice of you, General.

O'GORMAN. I said to Willie, "would ye like to stand for
Parliament?" Willie said, "Yes." " 'Twill cost ye a pretty
penny," I said to Willie. "That I haven't got," says Willie. "Me boy," says I, "we'll not deprive Ireland of your
services for the mere matter of a—*couple of thousand
pounds.*"

KATIE. How very generous of you.

O'GORMAN. I said to Willie, "As for me—I haven't a
penny to bless myself with—not a penny, not a penny."
But, said I to Willie, "There be plenty to open wide their

purses in such a cause and proud of the chance." That's what I said to Willie—"Proud of the chance. Sure no one would deprive Ireland of your services for the mere matter of money."

KATIE. Can he serve her two thousand pounds worth?

O'GORMAN. It's a bargain she's got this day in Willie.

O'SHEA. May I suggest, General, that you let me handle this.

O'GORMAN. Oh, certainly. [*He rises.*] Mrs. O'Shea, with your kind permission I'll light a cigar and smoke it on your beautiful terrace. Good luck, my boy. [*Exits Up Right.*]

KATIE. What does he mean?

O'SHEA. He means I'm let in for two thousand pounds.

KATIE. You.

O'SHEA. My election expenses—and his.

KATIE. Willie, where will you get it?

O'SHEA. Why do you suppose I've come to you?

KATIE. I have nothing. You know that.

O'SHEA. You can get plenty.

KATIE. I can't ask Aunt Ben again. She paid your debts only a few months ago. You promised then—

O'SHEA. Could I tell then I'd be going into Parliament?

KATIE. Oh, Willie.

O'SHEA. I've won political honor and distinction and all I get is "Oh, Willie."

KATIE. Aunt Ben has done enough for me.

O'SHEA. You've done plenty for her.

KATIE. I've done nothing.

O'SHEA. You're at her beck and call.

KATIE. She gave me this house. She wants me near her. She loves me.

O'SHEA. You earn your keep.

KATIE. [*Rises.*] Do you earn *your* keep, Willie?

O'SHEA. [*Rises. Crosses to her slowly.*] Yes, I do. I stay away from you, don't I?

KATIE. Yes, because you're paid to. I've asked you to divorce me—you won't. You use me to extort money, you humiliate me, you shame me.

O'SHEA. Shame you?

KATIE. I'm sorry, Willie, I don't want to quarrel.

O'SHEA. Shame you. What about me? What do you think I am? "Thanks for the election but you can whistle for the money." [*Crosses to her.*] That's what I'm to say, is it? I'll be the laughing stock of London. Talk of ashamed—I tell you I won't have it.

KATIE. [*Sits.*] It's no use, Willie. I've made up my mind.

O'SHEA. [*Looks at* KATIE. *Sits.*] Have you? I'm too good-natured. Most husbands wouldn't stand being without their wives for two years. I don't know how I have. I have rights around here, and by God—

KATIE. Willie—wait. I'm sorry.

O'SHEA. Will you get the money? Yes or no?

KATIE. I'll try.

O'SHEA. You can get it if you want to. Will you ask for it? Say yes or no.

KATIE. [*Faintly.*] Yes.

[*They break.*]

O'SHEA. Very well, will you send it to me in town or would you prefer me to come down here for it?

[*Pause.*]

ANNIE. [*Coming in from the garden, crosses Down Right Center.*] Katie— [KATIE *rises and crosses.*] Aunt Ben wants to know why you don't give the gentlemen tea?

KATIE. [*Crosses Up Right.*] Of course. How stupid of me.

O'SHEA. Annie.

ANNIE. How do you do, Willie?

KATIE. General. [O'GORMAN *enters.* KATIE *up to Right window.*] I want you to meet my sister Mrs. Steele.

Annie, this is General The O'Gorman Mahon. My sister, Mrs. Steele, General.

O'GORMAN. [*Bowing.*] Your servant, Madam.

KATIE. [*Crossing.*] Do have tea, General.

O'GORMAN. No tea, thank you.

ANNIE. But you must come and speak to my aunt, Mrs. Wood. She knew you, I believe, when she was Caroline O'Farrell.

O'GORMAN. Caroline O'Farrell. The toast of London and Dublin.

KATIE. [*Leading him to garden.*] She is in the garden, General. [*Moves toward the window and* O'GORMAN *follows her.*]

O'GORMAN. [*He goes out with* KATIE *reminiscing.*] The beautiful Caroline O'Farrell. It was in the year—

[KATIE *and* O'GORMAN *exit.*]

O'SHEA. [*Eagerly crossing to* ANNIE.] What luck—finding you here.

ANNIE. Luck! When I had your letter I decided to drive down.

O'SHEA. [*Crosses to her.*] You angel.

ANNIE. And—I'll drive you back.

O'SHEA. Marvellous. I'll get rid of The O'Gorman.

ANNIE. No. Better not. Aunt Ben has eyes like gimlets.

[*Back.*] Have you talked to Katie about entertaining for you yet?

O'SHEA. No.

ANNIE. You must. It's more important than ever, Willie, politically— And it will look so much better— for us.

O'SHEA. Having Katie around, you mean.

ANNIE. Of course.

O'SHEA. I'll make her. By God, if Katie were only like you—I wouldn't—

ANNIE. Yes, you would, Willie. You're no husband. Of *course* she doesn't understand you and all that sort of thing—

O'SHEA. Are you making fun of me?

ANNIE. But *I* do. I don't expect the model of all the virtues wrapped in the same package with curly blond hair, blue eyes—

O'SHEA. [*Seizing her and kissing her.*] And *this.*

ANNIE. Willie! Be careful! [*Disengaging herself— Crosses to Left Center chair.*] Suppose Aunt Ben, or Katie—

O'SHEA. [*Crosses to her.*] When can I see you alone then?

ANNIE. Don't be foolish, Willie.

O'SHEA. I tell you I won't be kept on toast this way. Herbert's away—I know he is. Let me come tonight.

ANNIE. [*Turns to him.*] Come to the house? Are you crazy? You know it's a hot-bed of governesses—children—servants—it isn't safe.

O'SHEA. You've got your feet firmly on the ground, haven't you, Annie?

ANNIE. I don't count the world well lost for love if that's what you mean—and you don't either—so let's be sensible.

O'SHEA. When am I to see you alone then?

ANNIE. [*After a pause.*] Are you invited to the Seymour Bellocs' the week-end of the twelfth?

O'SHEA. No—but I can get a bid. I know young Belloc.

ANNIE. You needn't. I'll ask Fannie to invite you. She will. I've been nice to her—on occasion.

O'SHEA. One good turn deserves another? All right then. It's a promise? You won't fail me? [ANNIE *moves to him and puts her hand against his cheek. He tries to kiss her but the same hand warns him back. A luscious smile to take the sting away.*] Annie—

ANNIE. Hush!

[AUNT BEN, *leaning on* O'GORMAN'S *arm and followed by* CLARA *and* KATIE, *comes in from the garden.*]

CLARA. [*Outside. In triumphantly righteous tones.*] I said the garden would be too damp—I was quite right.

AUNT BEN. [*Sits in chair Down Left Center.*] It isn't too damp. It's too cold.

[ANNIE *sits Right Center chair.*]

O'GORMAN. [*To* CLARA.] Your aunt should have a drop o' whisky. Nothin' so good for a chill.

AUNT BEN. Thank you, no, General—but *you* must have some.

O'GORMAN. You are most kind.

AUNT BEN. [*Sitting.*] Willie—

O'SHEA. How'd do, Aunt Ben?

AUNT BEN. Do give the General a whisky.

O'SHEA. [*Crosses Down Right to table.* O'GORMAN *follows* WILLIE.] Of course—let me—

AUNT BEN. Clara. Since the garden's so damp. You better go home and change your shoes.

CLARA. But, Aunt Ben—

AUNT BEN. Don't talk back.

O'SHEA. [*Pouring.*] Say "when."

O'GORMAN. [*With a loud laugh.*] Fill it up, man, and pour the rest of it over me. [*During the above lines* AUNT BEN *has said a few words to* CLARA *who leaves by the window.*] To high hopes. May they never fail us.

O'SHEA. Aunt Ben, you haven't congratulated me.

AUNT BEN. I do, Willie, I do.

O'SHEA. I mean to really go in for politics. I think I have a future.

AUNT BEN. Maybe—maybe.

O'SHEA. Some day I shall be Leader of the Irish Party —who knows!

O'GORMAN. Are you forgettin' Parnell?

O'SHEA. Forget! I voted for him, didn't I? And he never even thanked me.

O'GORMAN. Listen, Willie. Parnell doesn't have to thank anybody.

O'SHEA. If he thinks because he is the Leader of the Irish party—

KATIE. He *is* the Irish Party.

O'GORMAN. [*With quickening interest.*] Do you know him, Mrs. O'Shea?

KATIE. No.

ANNIE. [*Laughs.*] I met him once in the lobby of the house. The Irish Messiah impressed me as decidedly English.

AUNT BEN. He isn't. He was born in Ireland—educated here.

ANNIE. He's very reserved. I don't think he has much time for women.

O'GORMAN. That's because he's never laid eyes on Mrs. O'Shea.

KATIE. Thank you.

O'SHEA. We should entertain him, I think.

KATIE. Absurd. He can't be got by the most powerful political hostesses in London. Isn't that true, Annie?

ANNIE. You might try, Katie.

O'GORMAN. He'd not refuse you, my dear.

KATIE. How nice of you, General. Annie's impression doesn't give me much hope.

ANNIE. Don't be ridiculous. He's not invulnerable.

[O'GORMAN *replaces glass and returns to former position.*]

O'SHEA. Katie, it's important we at least try. I ought to give some political dinners.

ANNIE. You should if you want to get on.

O'GORMAN. Indeed, ye should cut a figure, Willie.

WILLIE. Will you help me, Katie? Invite Parnell to dine —act as hostess? It isn't much to ask.

O'GORMAN. I was wrong. You have a future, Willie.

O'SHEA. Well, Katie—

KATIE. But, Willie, don't you see he never—

O'GORMAN. Mrs. O'Shea, won't you plead the cause of two unworthies—that's you and me, Willie—

ANNIE. Hurry up and say yes, Katie. I must go and I want to hear the end of the story.

KATIE. What do you say, Aunt Ben?

AUNT BEN. Willie shouldn't be left cutting a figure alone.

O'SHEA. Will you, Katie?

KATIE. Very well, I'll ask him. Shall we set a time?

O'SHEA. I'll send you word immediately I get back to town. Thank you.

ANNIE. [*Turns to* O'SHEA—*back to audience.*] How delightful. [*Rises.*] Now, I simply must go. Willie, can't I give you and the General a lift to town?

[AUNT BEN *gives* KATIE *a look.*]

WILLIE. Awfully good of you.

O'GORMAN. It's delighted we'll be, Mrs. Steele.

ANNIE. I'll have to hurry you off I fear— [*Crosses to* AUNT BEN—*kisses them.*] I'm dining early. Goodbye, Aunt Ben. So lovely seeing you.

O'SHEA. [*Crosses to* AUNT BEN—*then crosses Up Right.*] Good afternoon, Aunt Ben.

AUNT BEN. Goodbye, Willie.

O'GORMAN. [*Turning, he bows over* AUNT BEN'S *hand and kisses it.*] More beautiful now as the evening star than even she was—

AUNT BEN. You better go, General, before that metaphor gets you into trouble.

O'GORMAN. As ever, your servant.

ANNIE. Don't forget you and Willie are going to dine with me? What about the tenth? Well—I'll see if Willie is free—and I'll have Herbert get tickets for the Lyceum. You'll come, won't you?

KATIE. I should love it.

ANNIE. Goodbye, General, I'm so glad you're driving back with me. The country is so lovely— [*She is way down the hall with* O'GORMAN.]

O'SHEA. About the other matter. You better send it to me in town. Make it soon. Goodbye. [*Exits.*]

AUNT BEN. [*To* KATIE, *after a pause.*] Well—how much does he want?

KATIE. Two thousand pounds.

AUNT BEN. What!

KATIE. Election expenses. His—and The O'Gorman's.

AUNT BEN. Willie's is not a timid nature.

KATIE. Oh, Aunt Ben, I'm so ashamed. So bitterly ashamed. I ought to fight Willie, alone.

AUNT BEN. [*Rises and crosses to her.*] You can't fight Willie alone. You can only get the best of him—sometimes. Katie, I'm dining here tonight.

KATIE. How adorable of you.

AUNT BEN. Not at all. You're having my favorite sweet. Clara won't let me eat it.

KATIE. Darling.

AUNT BEN. "Cutting a figure"! Humph! I'm not so sure it won't be worth two thousand pounds, after all.

CURTAIN

ACT ONE

SCENE II

SCENE—Committee Room, Number 15, House of Commons.
Doors Right and Left leading to small inner rooms. Door Center to the corridor. Fireplace Left.
TWO MEN are seated at a table. TIMOTHY HEALY has a book containing the names of members of the Irish Party, arranged by County.
THOMAS MURPHY has a similar book, the names arranged alphabetically.

MURPHY. [*Reading.*] Severn—S-e-v-e-r-n, Patrick, County Limerick.

HEALY. [*Turning to his County Book.*] Limerick— Limerick— [*Finds the page.*] Mr. Patrick Severn. [*Consults a small notebook and reads.*] "Good in a fight but no brains. One hundred pounds to Party funds. Can be trusted." [*He writes this in the County Book then looks up at Murphy.*]—"can be trusted"—all right —next.

MURPHY. [*Looking in own book.*] Shand— [*Spelling.*]

S-h-a-n-d, Mr. Timothy, County Mayo. [MURPHY *watching little book.*]

HEALY. Mayo—here it is—County Mayo. "Fifty pounds to Party funds. Obstinate as a mule. Brains. Can be trusted." [*Writes in the County Book.*]

MURPHY. [*Slowly.*] How does he know? That's what I can't get through my head.

HEALY. [*Disturbed in his writing.*] What?

MURPHY. Mr. Parnell? How does he know Severn and Shand can be trusted?

HEALY. [*Writing.*] He knows. You can stake your last quid.

MURPHY. He said of George Cobbe, "wouldn't trust with a bad six-pence."

HEALY. An' did you?

MURPHY. No.

HEALY. You were lucky, Murphy.

MURPHY. But how does he know so much?

HEALY. He can see right through to the back buttons on your braces. That's how. [*Writes rapidly.*] Go on.

MURPHY. [*Referring again to his list.*] Shea—S-h-e-a —County Clare.

HEALY. [*Looking in the County Book.*] Clare, County Clare—it's O'Shea, Murphy.

MURPHY. Mr. Healy, I took the liberty of discardin' the O's entirely. They filled the book. I alphabetted by the second letter for convenience.

HEALY. Damned inconvenient, if you ask me. Oh well —let's get on. "O'Shea, William Henry—

MURPHY. [*With a grin.*] *"Willie"* O'Shea.

[DAVITT *enters.*]

HEALY. Evening, Michael.

DAVITT. Evening. Where's Mr. Parnell?

HEALY. In the house, I suppose.

DAVITT. He told me to meet him here.

HEALY. Late—of course.

MURPHY. [*Smiling.*] Sure, it's important business he's got?

DAVITT. Of course, it's important.

MURPHY. An' didn't I just *say* important.

[DAVITT *walks Right.*]

HEALY. Shut up, Murphy.

MURPHY. [*Smothering his feelings and resuming the thread of conversation.*] William O'Shea.

HEALY. [*Looking at his notes.*] The Chief has no comment on him.

DAVITT. [*Stops and turns.*] Well, I have.

MURPHY. [*Imitating a man with a monocle and an English accent.*] "Oh, I say, me good man, have you seen me top hat?" [*His tone changing.*] And him by the name of O'Shea.

DAVITT. [*Crosses back.*] To hell with him.

MURPHY. [*Eagerly.*] To hell with him—write it down.

HEALY. Nothing goes in this book except on orders from the Chief.

MURPHY. Well, if he can see through to the back of yer pants it's eager I am for his word on O'Shea.

DAVITT. [*Looking at his watch.*] Before the sitting Mr. Parnell was tryin' to see Gladstone—but he won't.

MURPHY. And why not?

DAVITT. Because the old dog fox won't be caught—until he can't help himself.

MURPHY. Sure, he's no fox—it's a spider he is—waitin' to devour the Irish.

DAVITT. He'll be waitin' a long time I'm thinkin'.

MURPHY. Why should Mr. Parnell lower himself hangin' around the English? "No traffic with the enemy" That's my motto.

DAVITT. [*Turning on him.*] *Your* motto—burnin' an' outrage is your motto. An' how far have ye got with it? How near has Ireland been to gettin' Home Rule until now—*now*. This Party, that Party. It's all one to us if they'll give us what we want.

MURPHY. Why should they? They never have.

HEALY. Why should they? Are ye blind, man?

DAVITT. Count the new names, ye have the lists. Who'll be namin' the next Prime Minister? The Queen likely? I'll tell ye. Just one man.

MURPHY. [*Awed.*] Charles Stewart Parnell.

DAVITT. God love him.

HEALY. [*To* MURPHY. *Balancing imaginary scales.*] That Party—that Party—Parnell calls the tune.

DAVITT. [*Steps up. Hotly.*] It's hangin' round the English we are, is it? Well—the English'll be doin' the hangin' before long, or my name's not Michael Davitt.

HEALY. Never a word of this, Murphy. Mr. Parnell does his own talking.

MURPHY. Never a word.

[*The door from the corridor is flung wide by a young man, blue-eyed and with a boyish smile but he is not smiling at the moment. He is* MONTAGUE HARRISON, PARNELL'S *secretary, called "*MONTY.*"*]

MONTY. Gentlemen—the Irish members are being suspended from the House.

HEALY. Suspended? For what?

MONTY. For moving that Mr. Gladstone be no longer heard.

MURPHY. [*Overjoyed. To* HEALY.] Holy Mither! Tellin' the Old Spider to shut up.

MONTY. Gentlemen, Mr. Parnell says, will you please, all of you go down and get suspended, at once.

MURPHY. [*Jumping to his feet.*] Will I get suspended! [DAVITT *steps back.*] I'll get suspended—an' as soon as that's done—I'll refuse to *be* suspended. [*Crosses to Right door.*]

MONTY. [*Stops him.*] Mr. Parnell says no violence, please.

MURPHY. [*Dejected.*] An' did he that? Well—sittin' still's no violence. Devil a foot will I stir from the place till they get the police after me.

HEALY. Murphy—you put your motion—get suspended —and *come right back to these books.*

MURPHY. [*Sadly.*] Yes, Sir. [*He goes out.*]

DAVITT. [*Cross to end of table. To* MONTY.] Mr. Parnell started this, of course?

MONTY. Oh, yes, Sir. He was suspended over an hour ago.

DAVITT. We'd better be followin' Murphy, Mr. Healy. [*To* MONTY. *Finishing off writing.*] If Mr. Parnell comes, tell him where we are, will ye, Mr. Harrison?

MONTY. Yes, Mr. Davitt. He'll be here any minute. [HEALY *rises.*] He's in a great hurry for those lists.

HEALY. We won't be long.

[*The door from the corridor opens and* PARNELL *comes in. He is tall, dark-haired, slender, a man between thirty and thirty-five. Very pale, curiously burning dark eyes. His manner, unconsciously aloof is very quiet. The relation between himself and his Party workers is almost that of a schoolmaster, adored yet feared by his pupils.*]

PARNELL. Good evening, Gentlemen.

HEALY. Good evening, Chief.

DAVITT. [*Jubilant.*] We're on our way to get suspended, Mr. Parnell.

PARNELL. [*With his grave smile.*] That won't take you long, Michael.

DAVITT. Not if you're an Irish member, it won't.

PARNELL. Good luck.

[HEALY *and* DAVITT *exit.*]

MONTY. Murphy's gone, too. Mr. Parnell, when all our members have been suspended, what will happen, Sir?

PARNELL. Nothing. They'll take us all back in a day or two.

MONTY. But before they do—they'll pass the Coercion Bill, won't they, Sir?

PARNELL. Yes. In any case we can't stop that—now. But we can show them our strength—and unity.

MONTY. [*With enthusiasm.*] "Sit together, act together, *vote* together."

PARNELL. [*Nods. He walks over to the table and glances at the books.*] When the Grand Old Man sees us walking out "together," I think perhaps he will condescend to notice me.

MONTY. The Party's with you to a man, Sir.

PARNELL. [*Sits.*] There are no men in politics, Monty. Only votes— And secretaries.

MONTY. I'm a vote too, Sir, if I can vote for you. [*Mechanically.*] Oh Mr. Parnell, may I remind you of your appointment with Mr. Clarke at eleven o'clock tonight. Tomorrow morning at nine-thirty you are to see Mr. McLeanore and Mr. Martin to discuss Irish export. Lunch with—

PARNELL. [*He has been talking to* MONTY *but his inner mind has been concerning itself with a different train of thought.*] Monty—

MONTY. Yes, Sir.

PARNELL. Did you ever hear of a rose called the Queen's Messenger? It's white. Perhaps that isn't the real name —with a strange scent—heavy and white.

MONTY. [*Amazed.*] Yes, Sir. We used to grow them at home in Ireland.

PARNELL. I have not suddenly gone mad, Monty. I merely happened to—remember a rose. I'm still the

Leader of the Irish Party—and I still intend to get a Parliament for Ireland. Don't be alarmed.

[*The door opens and* MURPHY *comes in.*]

MURPHY. Good evenin', Sir.

PARNELL. Well, Murphy—how did it go?

[MONTY *makes notes in his book.*]

MURPHY. [*Resents.*] Very paceful, Sir. When I took me seat the old gentleman was spakin'. Pretty soon he thumps the table, so I thumps the bench and moves the Honorable Member be no longer heard, an' he says I'm suspended—an' I was. All very paceful.

PARNELL. Good. Thank you, Murphy.

MURPHY. When I left Mr. Healy was on his feet. He'll be baptized and back agin before you can say Jack Robinson. [*Sits.*]

PARNELL. How are the lists coming on?

MURPHY. We're nearly done, Sir. Just a few things Mr. Healy has to ask you, Sir. Sure it's wonderful, Mr. Parnell, all ye know about the members. It's afraid I am to read what's written under the name of Thomas Moonlight Murphy.

PARNELL. Turn to his name, Monty.

MURPHY. [*Hastily—scared.*] You needn't put yourself to that bother, Mr. Harrison.

MONTY. [*Turning the pages.*] Here it is. [*Looks up.*] "To be trusted."

MURPHY. [*Smiles. Then his face falls a little.*] And is there any word about "brains"?

MONTY. [*Reading.*] "Some brains—will learn." [*Puts down book and backs.*]

[DAVITT *and* HEALY *come in from the corridor.*]

HEALY. [*Crosses to former seat.*] Twenty have been suspended already, Mr. Parnell.

PARNELL. About fifty more to come. It will take them all night.

HEALY. [*Sits. With a smile.*] It will that.

PARNELL. Nice breathing spell for work.

DAVITT. Well—did you see the old man? Did ye see Gladstone?

PARNELL. No.

DAVITT. [*Indignantly.*] What word did he send ye?

PARNELL. None. I gather he's afraid to be seen with me publicly. Wants to be sure first what I can do for him. Well—I'm showing him.

DAVITT. He is the old spider.

PARNELL. But he'll not get any of my flies in his parlor, unless—

DAVITT. There's no unless.

PARNELL. [*Lightly.*] It's a very pretty parlor, Michael.

HEALY. I beg your pardon, Mr. Parnell. We've come to the name of O'Shea. You've nothing down for him.

PARNELL. [*Definitely.*] No.

HEALY. He voted for you.

DAVITT. [*At table.*] If he did less he'd be out of his wits.

HEALY. He ought to have influence.

DAVITT. He ought to be in prison. They say he's a friend of Chamberlain's.

PARNELL. He can't be imprisoned for that.

DAVITT. Some have for less.

PARNELL. I know that, Michael.

MONTY. [*Breaking in quite casually.*] *You've accepted several dinner invitations from the O'Sheas, Sir.*

PARNELL. What!

MONTY. Oh, you've never gone, Sir.

PARNELL. Not unless I walked in my sleep.

DAVITT. And might I ask who told you to accept anything from the O'Sheas?

MONTY. [*Defensively.*] I always accept invitations from the Party for Mr. Parnell. They know he won't come but it pleases the women. They can say he accepted and was—prevented.

PARNELL. I hadn't thought of O'Shea as being in the Party, yet.

DAVITT. He's not. He doesn't belong.

PARNELL. His vote does.

HEALY. [*Reading.*] "O'Shea. Captain William Henry." [*There is a knock at the door.* MONTY *crosses to answer it.*] No comment. But he'll vote with the boys I'm thinking.

DAVITT. Are ye now?

USHER. [*Outside.*] Someone to see Mr. Parnell.

DAVITT. He can't be seen. He's busy.

MONTY. Just a moment, please. [MONTY *crosses few steps into room.*] *Mrs.* William Henry O'Shea.

DAVITT. Speak of the devil—

HEALY. What can she want?

MURPHY. To invite him to dinner, old top.

MONTY. Do you want to see her, Mr. Parnell?

PARNELL. She's a friend of Gladstone's, isn't she?

MONTY. Yes, Sir.

PARNELL. [*Crossing before* DAVITT *to Right end of table.*] Will you ask Mrs. O'Shea to come in.

DAVITT. You're never going to see her, the wife of that—

PARNELL. [*Turning to* DAVITT.] I don't often ask advice. When I do, I take it. Murphy and Mr. Healy, supposing you take the books into the next room.

[HEALY *exits.* MURPHY *rises.*]

MURPHY. Yes, Mr. Parnell. I'd like to say, Sir, when you wrote the words "Can be trusted" under Tom Murphy's name, ye were writing God's truth.

PARNELL. [*With one of his grave smiles.*] Thank you, Murphy.

[MURPHY *exits up Left.*]

DAVITT. Mr. Parnell— [PARNELL *glares at him.*] Oh, very well. [DAVITT *exits up left.*]

[PARNELL *walks a few steps Left. He has his back to the door.* MRS. O'SHEA *enters door Right. She is charmingly dressed in a white evening dress. Her cloak is white and she wears a few white roses.*]

KATIE. [*Hesitating a moment*]—Mr. Parnell?

[PARNELL *turns to her. For a moment they look at each other as people might in a dream,—a sort of wondering intentness, not at all the sort of look one gives in London drawing rooms in the year 1880.* PARNELL *crosses to her without speaking.*]

PARNELL. Yes—and you?

KATIE. I sent in my card.

PARNELL. [*He looks at her as though only by an effort of will could he look away.*] *You* are—Mrs. O'Shea?

KATIE. Katharine O'Shea.

[PARNELL *holds out his hand almost mechanically, not the usual social gesture. She puts her hand in his.*]

PARNELL. You—! [*She withdraws her hand.*] I—I beg your pardon. But I have seen you before—the other night—in the lobby—do you remember?

KATIE. Yes.

PARNELL. You wore those white roses. There was a crowd and I lost you. Then tonight—while I was speaking—you came into the gallery.

KATIE. Yes. [*Then turning toward him in surprise.*] You can't see into the Ladies Gallery from the floor of the House.

PARNELL. No—but I knew. I was speaking and suddenly—I knew you were there. Don't think me mad.

KATIE. You are a little—aren't you?

PARNELL. Perhaps. Do you always wear white roses?

KATIE. They only bloom in June.

PARNELL. I shall have them grown all the year for you.

KATIE. Mr. Parnell—

PARNELL. I have been trying for days to find out who you were.

KATLE. Couldn't you? I'm not at all mysterious.

PARNELL. I found it difficult.—Could you tell me the name of a woman with dark hair—grey eyes— [*He can only look into them.*] Wearing white roses. [*He breaks off.*] I found it difficult.

KATIE. [*Summoning resolution.*] Mr. Parnell, you are quite mad—

PARNELL. Yes, if you like.

KATIE. I think I'd better go. [*She turns to go.*]

PARNELL. Don't go—please—have I offended you? I swear I won't again. I can be quite sane. You'll see I— I'll talk about the weather.

KATIE. Good night.

PARNELL. Did you see the Irish suspensions?

KATIE. I saw yours.

PARNELL. Amusing—wasn't it?

KATIE. No! I wanted to kill Gladstone.

PARNELL. Did you? How kind of you! Don't though. I hope he'll prove useful.

KATIE. I had a talk with him the other day. He was at my aunt's—Mrs. Wood. They are old friends. I asked him outright if he was a friend of yours—and of Ireland's. He said— [*She pauses.*] At great length and with much elaboration—nothing at all.

PARNELL. [*Gaily.*] He does it so well, too.

KATIE. Doesn't he!

PARNELL. In the House last night he made an impassioned speech—whether for or against us—God knows.

KATIE. How disappointing!

PARNELL. Oh, no. I had the Irish members cheer loudly —so everyone thought he was for us.

KATIE. [*Eagerly but with dread in her voice.*] Oh, Mr. Parnell—I hope *you* will not prove useful to him.

PARNELL. I assure you, if he does swallow me up, I shall be a very nasty mouthful.

[*She looks—turns to go.*]

KATIE. It was suggested that I—

PARNELL. Yes?

KATIE. Never mind—good night.

PARNELL. [*Crosses and gives hand.*] I shall see you again.

KATIE. No.

PARNELL. When shall I see you again?

KATIE. Mr. Parnell, my husband is one of the new members of your Party.

PARNELL. Yes—I know.

KATIE. [*Quietly.*] I shall not see you again.

PARNELL. [*Levelly.*] You know that is not true. It can never be true in this world.

KATIE. Oh, don't—don't.

PARNELL. I have known you always.

KATIE. [*Steadily.*] We have met tonight—for the first time.

PARNELL. In a Committee Room of the House of Commons, London—but not for the first time. [*Crosses, breaks hand clasp.*]

KATIE. I should never have come here.

PARNELL. Why did you come?

KATIE. [*Pause.*] It doesn't matter.

PARNELL. No—not now.

[KATIE *crosses to the door. He watches her quietly. He knows he has found her. As she moves a rose falls from her dress. With her hand on the knob she turns and looks at him. Such a look Eurydice must have given Orpheus.* PARNELL *crosses to her and lays his hand on her bare arm. She gives a shivering sigh of ecstasy and looks up at him*].

KATIE. Good night. [KATIE *exits.*]

[PARNELL *stands looking after her.* DAVITT *enters door Up Left.*]

DAVITT. Excuse me. She's gone.

PARNELL. Yes.

DAVITT. She didn't stay long.

PARNELL. No.

DAVITT. I don't suppose she asked you again for dinner.

PARNELL. No— [*He crosses back to table, and sits in former seat.*] but I'm going.

DAVITT. You're going?

PARNELL. If God lets me.

DAVITT. You're daft I'm thinkin'.

PARNELL. I'm thinking so too. [*He rings bell.*] Monty.

[MONTY *enters door Right.*]

CURTAIN

ACT ONE

Scene III

SCENE—*Drawing room at Eltham.*
A lamp is burning. The stage is empty.
Laughter is heard from across the hall. KATIE
enters from door on Right, crosses stage and
sits on chair Down Left. After looking out
Upper Left window, O'SHEA *enters hurriedly.*

O'SHEA [*Crossing Center.*] Well, Katie!

KATIE. Was everything as you liked it?

O'SHEA. Yes. Your dinners are always perfect, Mrs.
O'Shea.

KATIE. I'm glad this one was. Cook has been in a trance
for days at the prospect, and Phyllis and Delia are
stricken dumb with joy. Being in the actual *presence*.

O'SHEA. Is that what's the matter with you?

KATIE. [*Rises.*] Was I dumb?

O'SHEA. Yes, what's wrong with you? You can be gay
enough when you want to be. Not a word to say for
yourself. What's the matter? Most women go wild over
him.

47

KATIE. He doesn't over them apparently.

O'SHEA. Oh, is that it. He doesn't pay enough compliments. Well—he's interested. I can tell you that.

KATIE. Willie, please.

O'SHEA. Don't spoil things with your damned airs. Why did you clear out?

KATIE. It's usual to leave the gentlemen to their wine, isn't it?

O'SHEA. Don't make stupid evasions. I begged you to stay. We all did, but no, you swept out like a Siddons.

KATIE. You asked me to entertain Mr. Parnell as part of your political program. Well, I have. If the result is not what you hoped I'm sorry but I can't help it.

O'SHEA. Maybe you're playing the game after all. Leadin' him on? Well, take a bit of advice. Don't give him too much line. He might jump off your hook.

[PHYLLIS *enters.*]

KATIE. Don't you think you should return to your guests?

O'SHEA. Not a bad idea. [O'SHEA *exits.*]

[KATIE *sits down at the piano.* PHYLLIS *crosses to draw curtains on window Up Left, after putting down decanter and glasses on table behind settee Down Right.*]

KATIE. Don't draw the curtains, Phyllis.

PHYLLIS. Yes, Ma'am, but it's dark outside.

KATIE. Is the twilight all gone?

PHYLLIS. [*Crosses to Right window.*] It's dark as hope and the moon not up till late.

KATIE. Very well. [PHYLLIS *pulls the curtains. She crosses to Right door.*] The dinner was nice, Phyllis. Please tell Cook.

PHYLLIS. Yes, Ma'am. I never thought to see the day I'd wait on Mr. Parnell. Delia and me is both writin' home about it. Delia's doin' the writin' for us both, mine bein' what it is. That is unless, [*Closer.*] you'll excuse me, Ma'am—

KATIE. What is it, Phyllis?

PHYLLIS. I thought, Ma'am, if it wouldn't be puttin' ye to too much trouble— It's yourself might be afther writin' to me mither for me—makin' the letters very plain, please, Ma'am—as it's Mr. Parnell I'm tellin' her about.

KATIE. Is your mother one of Mr. Parnell's admirers?

PHYLLIS. It's worships the ground he walks on, she does. Sure, he's the uncrowned king of Ireland. And if you'll be afther makin' the letters very plain. Delia's writin' is not what she thinks it is, if you're askin' me.

KATIE. I'll make them very plain, Phyllis.

PHYLLIS. Thank you, Ma'am. [*She crosses Down Right to sofa.* PARNELL *enters.* KATIE *stops playing.*]

PARNELL. Don't stop.

KATIE. Phyllis, will you tell Captain O'Shea and The O'Gorman Mahon that I should be glad to see them in the drawing room.

PHYLLIS. Yes, Ma'am.

KATIE. I think a game of whist might be pleasant— Tell Captain O'Shea.

PHYLLIS. Yes, Ma'am. [PHYLLIS *exits.*]

PARNELL. Why did you stop? Please go on.

KATIE. [*Rises—crosses to him.*] It's too sad.

PARNELL. A wail for the dead.

KATIE. Don't say that. It's a bad omen.

PARNELL. Do you believe in omens?

KATIE. Do you?

PARNELL. Yes.

KATIE. They can't have any influence—really. They can't change things.

PARNELL. Nothing can change Fate—

KATIE. They can point to it?

PARNELL. The Ides of March you know.

KATIE. I don't believe in destiny—or predestined Fate.

PARNELL. Yet you try to escape it. You wouldn't drive with me yesterday. Why?

KATIE. [*Crosses to settee Down Right.*] I had another engagement.

PARNELL. [*Following Down.*] You're avoiding me.

KATIE. That's absurd.

PARNELL. Is it?

KATIE. Why should I avoid you?

PARNELL. [*At chair.*] Shall I tell you?

KATIE. [*Sits.*] No.

PARNELL. Then will you tell me why you wouldn't drive with me?

KATIE. The reason's obvious.

PARNELL. You didn't care to.

KATIE. Is that obvious? I should have said that was conventional.

PARNELL. Do conventions mean so much to you?

KATIE. They mean nothing to me. But they do to others. I hoped you wouldn't come here tonight.

PARNELL. You knew that I would.

KATIE. I hoped that you would see that it was—

PARNELL. Unwise? Oh, yes—I saw that—perfectly— with my House of Commons vision.

KATIE. And yet—you came.

PARNELL. There is another vision— It comes only once

—sometimes never—that moment when the heavens open—and there is light. I've seen it.

KATIE. Don't.

PARNELL. [*Sits in chair.*] Can't we at least be honest.

KATIE. No.

PARNELL. I will have nothing else.

KATIE. Very well. Willie asked you here tonight hoping you would find me attractive. Attractive enough to pull some political plums into Willie's mouth. It was a trap —and you've fallen into it.

PARNELL. Not fallen—jumped. O'Shea is fairly transparent. But what has that to do with me?

[*The door opens and* O'SHEA *and* O'GORMAN *come in.* PHYLLIS *follows and waits to see if she is wanted further.*]

O'SHEA. —And now General here's a chance to prove your game.

O'GORMAN. How much a point?—Mrs. O'Shea, when I was in France they used to tell me I was the only man who knew where and when to finesse.

O'SHEA. Shall we play in the library, it's cozier.

O'GORMAN. And a shorter reach for the glass I'm thinking.

KATIE. Phyllis—we will play in the library.

PHYLLIS. Yes, Ma'am. [PHYLLIS *goes out.*]

PARNELL. [*Smiling.*] I'm very sorry but I never played a hand in my life.

O'SHEA. [*Staring at* KATIE.] A joke of Katie's perhaps.

KATIE. I—misunderstood Mr. Parnell.

O'SHEA. [*Crosses to left Center chair—turns it. Pulling his mustache.*] Quite so. A chat will be pleasanter all round, I think. Will you sit here, General?

PARNELL. [*Rises.*] It is getting late. I must say good night.

O'GORMAN. Sure the shank of the evenin's still to come.

PARNELL. I speak in the House tomorrow and still have some preparation to make.

O'SHEA. Mr. Parnell, will Ireland ever really get a Parliament?

PARNELL. Yes. Sooner or later.

KATIE. If anything happened to you it would be later. Perhaps too late.

PARNELL. Perhaps, but it is already written.

KATIE. Not yet. We are writing it now.

PARNELL. The book is shut.

O'GORMAN. Faith I'd like to look ahead a page or two. It's a bomb I'd put under old Gladstone and all his shilly-shally-shenanigin—off again—on again—gone again Finnegan.

O'SHEA. He's a hard one to pin down.

PARNELL. I'll pin him down or—

O'SHEA. [*Too eagerly.*] Or what?

PARNELL. Or—I won't.

O'SHEA. What does he say?

PARNELL. Nothing. I can't reach him.

O'SHEA. I know one who could.

O'GORMAN. Is it yourself you're meanin', Willie?

O'SHEA. I'm not pious enough for that old bird. But Katie—he dotes on Katie.

KATIE. Oh, no. I'm not pious either, Willie.

O'SHEA. He hasn't found that out yet. Katie's your bet, Mr. Parnell.

PARNELL. [*To* KATIE.] Will you, Mrs. O'Shea?

KATIE. I know nothing of politics.

PARNELL. I *need* someone whose discretion *is* absolute. Someone I can trust.

KATIE. Can you trust me?

PARNELL. Utterly.

O'GORMAN. With such a teacher as Mr. Parnell, you go far. We ought to be goin'. We're forever catching boats or trains.

o'shea. [*Looking at his watch.*] We just have time to make the last one.

parnell. Sorry my trap only holds two.

o'shea. So you drove down?

parnell. I dislike trains.

o'shea. Will you allow me to make my excuses and leave first, Mr. Parnell?

[katie *rises, crosses Up.*]

parnell. Certainly.

o'shea. You were very good to come to us for so informal an evening.

parnell. Not at all. I go nowhere for formal ones.

o'shea. Good night. I shall see you tomorrow at the House.

parnell. Good night and thank you.

katie. [*To* o'gorman.] Good night, General.

o'gorman. Good night, Mrs. O'Shea. A delightful evening. I kiss your hand.

All together.

katie. Perhaps, Mr. Parnell would drive you up to London, even if he hadn't room for Willie.

o'gorman. County Clare sticks together. I'll not be desertin' Willie. [*Crosses to* parnell.] Good night to ye, Mr. Parnell.

[O'GORMAN *exits.*]

O'SHEA. Good night, Katie. Good night, Parnell. See you tomorrow. [O'SHEA *exits.*]

PARNELL. [*Crosses Center to her.*] They were embarrassingly obvious but I bless their departure. [*Crosses a step to her.*]

KATIE. Please go.

PARNELL. Are you afraid of the truth? I love you.

KATIE. No—no, it's not true.

PARNELL. I love you.

KATIE. You shall not say it. I ask you not to.

PARNELL. A man sees a woman for a moment—and he loves her. Is there anything more to be said?

KATIE. So much.

PARNELL. What?

KATIE. Ireland, will she live or die?

PARNELL. Ireland will live. My part in her life is settled. I love you. That is settled too. I'm not asking you to start a flirtation or even an affair. I want you before the world—my wife.

KATIE. You would have no world.

PARNELL. You're not living with O'Shea—all London knows that. He will divorce you.

KATIE. Not if it pays him to keep me. Don't you suppose

I have begged for a divorce? But if he should—then what of you? The Irish Messiah married to a divorced woman.

PARNELL. You are free— You are living apart—

KATIE. Oh, don't underestimate Willie. Every peasant from Ulster to Galway would be told you had stolen his wife. They would weep with him and turn on you and curse you.

PARNELL. All you say may be true—but it doesn't matter.

KATIE. Don't.

PARNELL. My darling, you are coming with me.

KATIE. No.

PARNELL. That night when I first saw you—the scent of the rose you wore swept over me—for that moment you were in my arms, my lips on yours. I knew I would never let you go. You are so beautiful—so beautiful. [*Taking her in his arms.*] I love you. [*Kisses.*]

KATIE. I should break your life.

PARNELL. Then it's broken.

KATIE. Your life, for a passing moment, a woman—

PARNELL. The scent of a rose. Oh, my sweet—my sweet—can you leave me now?

KATIE. [*On his shoulder.*] Don't let me go. Never let me go.

PARNELL. You will come with me?

KATIE. I can't—because I love you—but I can't let you go. You must come to me. Oh, my darling, will you come to me?

PARNELL. I shall come where you are—always.

[*Kisses.*]

CURTAIN

ACT TWO

ACT TWO

Scene I

Scene—*The drawing room at Eltham.*
It is Spring once more and afternoon sunshine streams in the windows. A woman's writing table and also a large desk table have been added to the room. Both are littered with documents, blue books, etc.
MONTAGUE HARRISON *comes in, a number of letters in his hand and newspapers under his arm. He is putting the letters on the large desk when the door opens and* PHYLLIS *shows in* AUNT BEN *and* CLARA.

AUNT BEN. [*Seeing* MONTY.] Good afternoon, Mr. Harrison. Are we interrupting?

PHYLLIS. [*To* AUNT BEN.] Excuse me. Mr. Harrison I thought Mrs. O'Shea was in here. I'll see where she is, Ma'am. [*Crosses and exits Up Left below desk.*]

MONTY. [*Conscious of being pumped.*] Please come in, Mrs. Wood. [*Bows.*] Miss Wood.

AUNT BEN. [*Crosses to sofa.*] You're quite sure we're not interrupting your work?

MONTY. Not at all. I'm working in my office this afternoon.

CLARA. [*Glancing at the larger desk.*] And we shall not be keeping Mr. Parnell from his desk?

MONTY. Mr. Parnell is in town this afternoon. [*Crosses behind desk.*]

[AUNT BEN *sinks into a chair.*]

CLARA. Ah! I saw him this morning taking his usual canter. He is keeping his horses down here now, isn't he?

MONTY. [*Briefly.*] Yes.

CLARA. He keeps himself fit in spite of the pressure of political life. So wise!

MONTY. If you will excuse me, I shall get back to my work. [*Crosses to Right door and is turned.*]

CLARA. You must be awfully busy. Fancy being secretary to the man who made Gladstone Prime Minister. Something to remember all one's life.

MONTY. Yes. Excuse me. [*He bows and goes out.*]

CLARA. Nice, chatty boy.

AUNT BEN. You didn't expect him to burst into confidences, did you? Your methods are so obvious, Clara. To lure political secrets requires finesse—not a frontal attack.

CLARA. [*Crosses to Down Left chair.*] I'm not interested in political secrets.

AUNT BEN. Nor am I.

CLARA. [*She is at chair and sits.*] But I am interested in other aspects of this affair which are neither political nor secret.

AUNT BEN. Clara, will you be kind enough to open a window. This room seems warm. [CLARA *crosses to open a window Up Right.*] Fancy—a fire this late in May.

CLARA. Mr. Parnell no doubt likes warm rooms.

AUNT BEN. And will you oblige me by not making any further allusions to Mr. Parnell. I am tired of the subject.

CLARA. [*Crossing back.*] So am I.

AUNT BEN. You have a strange way of showing it.

CLARA. [*Returns and sits.*] Tired of the whispers—the underground rumors—

AUNT BEN. [*Shutting her up.*] Very unusual this May. I can scarcely remember a season like it.

CLARA. Oh, Aunt Ben, why will you always put me off?

AUNT BEN. The state of the weather is of great interest to me, Clara. I can only get out when it's fine.

CLARA. I should think what people are saying about Katie would be of interest to you.

AUNT BEN. Not in the least.

CLARA. Well, you'll have to hear it—sooner or later, and I feel that I should prepare you.

AUNT BEN. You needn't trouble yourself. I am in full possession of my wits, though aged.

CLARA. Parnell practically lives here.

AUNT BEN. At Willie's invitation—as Willie's guest.

CLARA. They've pulled the wool over Willie's eyes, too. Can't you see? Why, you've only to look at them together—

AUNT BEN. I've heard enough.

CLARA. You've heard nothing because you won't. Not just London but all Ireland is seething with it.

[KATIE *has opened the door and is standing on the threshold. She is dressed in a "tea gown" or the "hostess" gown of the '80's.*]

AUNT BEN. I tell you, I've heard enough.

[KATIE *enters followed by* PHYLLIS, *who is carrying a black bag.*]

KATIE. [*As she enters, she is crossing to* AUNT BEN *and sits beside her.*] Darling, Aunt Ben, forgive my keeping you waiting. Put it by the desk, Phyllis. I've been cutting out the editorials of Mr. Parnell's last speech.

AUNT BEN. The papers are full of it.

KATIE. Wasn't it wonderful? Wasn't he wonderful? That was a hostile audience too. You know he has a way when odds are against him of throwing back his head and straightening his shoulders. Monty says that the boys at headquarters call it "Shoot and be damned."

CLARA. Asking for trouble—I wonder he has time to bother with Home Rule for the Irish with his many duties here.

KATIE. Mr. Parnell came here, Clara, at Willie's request after his serious illness nine months ago. We felt the country better for him, and that he needed personal attention.

CLARA. I'm sure he got it. It was something to do with his heart, no doubt.

KATIE. Yes.

CLARA. You hear it on all sides.

AUNT BEN. Be quiet.

KATIE. [*Crosses to Down Right desk.*] Let her speak, Aunt Ben. She's been bursting with it for days.

CLARA. I'm not the only one, I can tell you. Do you suppose others have not commented on Mr. Parnell's prolonged visits to Eltham these last few months?

KATIE. You're forgetting that Willie and I are also working with Mr. Parnell politically. Everyone knows that. [*Sits.*] Willie has just been re-elected to Parliament through Mr. Parnell's influence.

CLARA. And would you like to hear what Ireland has to say about that? What they are openly shouting at political meetings? [KATIE *stares at her terrified*.] Did you think you could have this man here most of the time— why he's even stabling his horses here, all the village knows that—yet you dare sit there and tell me he's nothing to you.

KATIE. [*Turns to* CLARA.] I'm not obliged to tell you anything, Clara. I'm not accountable to you.

CLARA. You can hedge if you want to but you can't fool me. I'm not a child—or a doting old woman.

KATIE. [*Rises.*] How *dare* you!

CLARA. I don't pretend to be the favorite niece. Oh, dear no—but I've never brought scandal on the family name—

AUNT BEN. [*Rises.*] No. You have been more than discreet, Clara, whether from choice or necessity I'm not prepared to say. I know you will be glad to shake from your skirts the contaminating dust of this house, so will you please go?

CLARA. Certainly. [*Starts to go.*] I have no desire to stay.

AUNT BEN. [*Crosses to Left Center chair.*] Oblige me by [*She stops moving.*] asking Morton to pack your boxes as quickly as possible. [CLARA *turns.*] As you are so particular about dust I think you'd better shake mine too.

CLARA. [*With a gasp.*] Aunt Ben! [*Crosses back to chair.*]

AUNT BEN. Oh, I shall continue your allowance. Indeed I shall increase it as you will no longer be living under my roof. Goodbye.

CLARA. I might have known what would happen.

AUNT BEN. Yes, the wicked flourish, Clara. That always seemed to surprise King David too. Goodbye. Be sure to leave your address with Morton.

CLARA. I shall be at Thomas' Hotel, London, of course.

AUNT BEN. That's an extremely respectable refuge.

CLARA. [*Starts to the door, turns then to* KATIE.] I hope you are satisfied. [*She goes out.* AUNT BEN *sits.*]

KATIE. I'm sorry, Aunt Ben, sorry this happened.

AUNT BEN. I've seen it coming. No one can stop Clara once her tongue begins to clack. It's all a pack of lies.

KATIE. Aunt Ben— [AUNT BEN *rests on her cane and looks searchingly at* KATIE.] It's all true.

AUNT BEN. I've known that for a long time, my dear.

KATIE. [*Crosses to* AUNT BEN.] You've—oh, Aunt Ben —Aunt Ben. [*She flings herself into* AUNT BEN'S *arms and they cling together.*]

AUNT BEN. [*Sighs, then after a pause.*] I told you that the wind outside would blow plenty of stones and dirt.

KATIE. Yes.

AUNT BEN. I hope the smell of earth and sea makes up for it. Does it?

KATIE. [*With a smile that Joan of Arc might have envied.*] Yes.

AUNT BEN. Katie—I'm afraid—for you.

KATIE. You mean because of Willie, I know, but in a little while he won't matter. Charles and I are going away.

AUNT BEN. In the next world, thank God, there will be no marrying or giving in marriage. The Lord himself sees it is a mistake. Well—ask one of the maids to walk across the park with me. I must get home before Clara has the entire house staff in hysterics.

[*There is a knock at the door.* KATIE *steps Down Left.*]

KATIE. [*Rises.*] Come in.

MONTY. Sorry. [*Coming in.*] This telegram has just come for you, Mrs. O'Shea.

KATIE. [*Takes the envelope and tears it open.*] Excuse me.

AUNT BEN. Mr. Harrison, [MONTY *takes steps Down.*] will you be good enough to ring?

[KATIE *crosses Up.* MONTY *crosses Down Left and pulls the bell rope.*]

KATIE. It's from Willie! He is coming down this afternoon.

MONTY. Mr. Parnell had a message from him too. Captain O'Shea crossed from Ireland last night.

AUNT BEN. I hear he's been re-elected

KATIE. By a small majority unfortunately.

MONTY. But we got him in. Did you know the other night

after the Sitting there was an Irishman waiting to kill him.

[KATIE *turns Up. Puts down telegram.*]

KATIE. To kill Willie?

AUNT BEN. [*Without emphasis.*] Who stopped him?

MONTY. Nobody. He was too drunk to kill anyone. He said the Captain had mocked him.

PHYLLIS. [*At the door.*] Did you ring, Ma'am.

[AUNT BEN *rises.*]

KATIE. Will you walk across the park with Mrs. Wood, please.

[PHYLLIS *crosses Up to Garden door.* KATIE *helps her.*]

AUNT BEN. [*Moving to the door.*] Congratulate Willie for me.

KATIE. On his election.

AUNT BEN. On his being alive. [*She goes out with* PHYLLIS *ad libbing.*]

KATIE. Monty, I'm going to ask you something and I want a straight answer.

MONTY. Yes?

KATIE. Was there any trouble at this last election?

MONTY. Did you ever hear of a peaceful Irish election?

KATIE. I mean, special trouble—about—Captain O'Shea?

MONTY. [*Evading.*] Well, you know how unpopular he is?

KATIE. I'm not going to get a straight answer, am I?

MONTY. Why—

KATIE. Oh, never mind. I'm being awkward. Has the post come?

MONTY. I put the letters on the desk.

[KATIE *crosses to desk.* MONTY *exits.* KATIE *crosses Up to* PARNELL'S *desk, looking at the mail.* PARNELL *enters thru Upper Right window.*]

PARNELL. [*Kisses her on neck.*] Queenie.

KATIE. Husband. [*They kiss.* PARNELL *crosses to piano stool and puts hat there.*] What brings you home so early —a guilty conscience?

PARNELL. [*Crosses back.*] A what?

KATIE. [*Points to bag.*] Don't try to look so injured. I'm very annoyed.

PARNELL. Where did you find it?

KATIE. Where you hid it.

PARNELL. You shouldn't pry.

KATIE. Why didn't you take it?

PARNELL. Because, my Beloved, the papers feared that it contained dynamite to blow up the Liberals should they fail to support Home Rule. I didn't want to worry them.

KATIE. This is no joke. What's the use of going to a Doctor if you won't obey him?

PARNELL. He never mentioned black bags.

KATIE. But he did mention dry shoes. Sir Harvey Wilson warned you—

PARNELL. I can't see the connection between a heart attack and getting one's feet wet.

KATIE. He said when you caught cold it affected your heart.

PARNELL. So I have to carry dry shoes wherever I go. Ridiculous.

KATIE. It wasn't so ridiculous last year when you were so terribly ill. [*Crosses to him.*] Do we have to go over all that again? Will you promise me to always take it with you. If you won't do it for me, will you do it for Ireland—and if you won't do it for Ireland, will you do it for me? And if you won't do it for either of us, I want you to move out of my house.

PARNELL. [*Crosses and gets bag.*] I don't want to move —so I promise.

KATIE. Sweet. [*She kisses him.*]

PARNELL. [*Crosses to her.*] You know, darling, only two things affect my heart—Home Rule and you. [*Kisses her.*]

KATIE. [*Crosses to sofa and lies down.*] I'm so glad you've come.

PARNELL. [*Follows.*] Anything wrong?

KATIE. No. Just glad. What are you doing here so early! Did you talk with Mr. Gladstone?

PARNELL. He is arranging a houseparty at Hawarden— to celebrate—

KATIE. [*She comes forward— Breathless.*] Home Rule! [*She kisses him.*] Darling.

PARNELL. He has promised to introduce it this Session.

KATIE. And I'm the first to know.

PARNELL. Oh, no. I told the butler as I came out, and several policemen who were standing around. They were *so* pleased and sent you their love. Darling, I could never have done it without your help. The Old Spider said as much today. He spoke of your "invaluable services." He wants you and Mrs. Wood to come to Hawarden three weeks next Thursday.

KATIE. *I!!*

PARNELL. [*Quickly.*] Why not!

KATIE. Well—of course he knows—he must know— about—us. It *is* rather nice of him.

PARNELL. Nice! God!!

KATIE. Oh, very well, darling, he'll probably put down a red carpet for me. Think of it—within three weeks. At any rate this means he is going through with it. Doesn't it?

PARNELL. I suppose so.

KATIE. Even Gladstone would hardly arrange a house-party—

PARNELL. Somehow I have the feeling that he is—waiting—

KATIE. For what?

PARNELL. [*Minimizes the count—not quite believing.*] To find the Ace of Trumps up his sleeve. I don't mind his finding the Ace of Trumps up his sleeve if he only wouldn't proclaim God Almighty put it there.

KATIE. [*Gives a little laugh.*] Did he congratulate you on your speech?

PARNELL. Soft soap.

KATIE. You were wonderful.

PARNELL. Was I?

KATIE. [*Quoting.*] "The English Government has wept over the sorrows of the Bulgars and the Armenians— will it never weep for the starving agony of Ireland?"

[*She breaks off smiling.*]

PARNELL. He was chief mourner for the Armenians, too. Rather decent of him to congratulate me.

KATIE. I was so proud of you.

PARNELL. I had one terrible moment, Katie, complete panic.

KATIE. [*Softly.*] Yes, I know.

PARNELL. I couldn't find you in the crowd. I thought "if I never find her." Utterly foolish. I know. Then your eyes looked into mine. I could go on. I love you. I wish I could find a new way of saying it.

KATIE. I shouldn't like a new way. I should simply hate it.

PARNELL. Katie— [*Leans back.*] as soon as Home Rule is safe—

KATIE. It is safe, darling.

PARNELL. Then—you and I, together—no more fencing, no more evasions—you and I—

KATIE. Where there's sunshine—

PARNELL. We shall soak in it.

KATIE. Italy—or Spain—

PARNELL. Or Algiers or Carcasonne. Soon—come soon— [*He takes her in his arms and kisses her.*]

KATIE. [*Simply.*] Oh, God—give us that day.

PARNELL. And millions more.

KATIE. Not millions. I should be tottering and horrible to look upon by then.

PARNELL. I don't insist on having them all in this world.

KATIE. It's the only one we're sure of.

PARNELL. [*Romantic.*] Don't be so local, darling. There's aeons and aeons of worlds. With you in each one.

KATIE. "Aeons." Such a lovely word.

PARNELL. Not if you are there. [*There is a knock on the door.* PARNELL *kisses her and releases her— Rises.*] Come in.

[*It is* MONTY *and he is obviously worried.*]

MONTY. [*Quivering.*] I didn't know you were here, Sir —but—Michael Davitt is here.

PARNELL. [*Absolutely still.*] What?

MONTY. I gave him no appointment, Mr. Parnell.

PARNELL. Send him away. You know I never see the Party here.

MONTY. Yes, Sir—but he seems a good deal upset. [*He glances at* MRS. O'SHEA.]

KATIE. [*Getting feet down.*] Perhaps you'd better see him.

PARNELL. Certainly not.

KATIE. [*Anxiously.*] Michael Davitt would never have come here unless his business were urgent. Won't you see him.

PARNELL. No.

KATIE. [*In a little rush of emotion.*]—Please.

PARNELL. [*After a pause.*] Monty—you may ask him to come in. [MONTY *goes.* PARNELL, *gently turns.*] What is it?

KATIE. [*Crosses to him. Hurriedly.*] Aunt Ben and Clara have just been here. Clara made a scene.

PARNELL. A scene?

KATIE. [*Warningly.*] She said all Ireland was talking about—you and me.

PARNELL. I'm sorry you had to know.

KATIE. It's true then. That's why you went to Ireland.

PARNELL. Yes. *Healy and Davitt refused to support O'Shea. I forced him down their throats.*

KATIE. [*Crosses up and down.*] Willie's coming here today to see you. I had a telegram.

PARNELL. [*Reads it—folds it—looks. Hands it to* KATIE *on speech. Definitely.*] I'm done with him, Katie.

KATIE. But, darling, be careful.

PARNELL. I ran him for Galway because you begged it of me.

KATIE. I was afraid.

PARNELL. He can never again say I have promised and not performed. But there comes an end to all things. I'm done with him.

KATIE. Whatever you do, don't anger him.

[MONTY *enters.* DAVITT *enters.*]

MONTY. Mr. Michael Davitt.

[DAVITT *is awkward and ill-at-ease. Strides in—awk-*

ward before KATIE. *He stands twirling his hat in his hands.*]

PARNELL. Come in, Michael. You know Mrs. O'Shea.

[MONTY *shuts door.*]

KATIE. [*Crosses to him.*] How do you do, Mr. Davitt? [*Stretches hand—he bows.*]

DAVITT. [*Coldly.*] Your servant, Ma'am.

KATIE. [*Crosses a step Up left. To* PARNELL.] I hope you'll ask Mr. Davitt to stay for tea, Charles.

DAVITT. Thank you kindly, Ma'am, but I'll be goin'.

KATIE. I am sorry. [*She moves to the door.*] Good afternoon. I'll be in the study if you want me. [KATIE *exits Upper Left.*]

DAVITT. Good afternoon, Ma'am.

[*She goes out followed by* MONTY *who closes the door into the hall after him. The two men look at each other for a moment.* MICHAEL'S *face is distressed, yet stubbornly obstinate.*]

PARNELL. [*Crosses to chair in front of desk. Coldly.*] Well? I suppose you have good reason for coming down here.

DAVITT. I have that.

PARNELL. Entirely against orders.

DAVITT. [*Anxiously.*] Mr. Parnell—haven't I always obeyed orders?

PARNELL. Yes. [*Sits.*]

DAVITT. Didn't I obey orders in this last election when I'd sooner cut off my right hand.

PARNELL. You were absolutely loyal, Michael.

DAVITT. [*Real insubordination.*] And so I am now, but I've come to tell you there'll be no more obeyin' orders if—what's goin' on isn't brought to an end.

PARNELL. [*Rises. His eyes blazing—towering temper.*] What do you mean?

DAVITT. [*Doggedly—tone down.*] I mean if there's any more favors goin' to Captain O'Shea.

PARNELL. [*Same.*] That is for me to say.

DAVITT. [*Pleadingly—tone apologizes.*] I know that. All I ask is that you hear me before it comes to the sayin'.

PARNELL. Go on.

DAVITT. [*Anxious for situation— At desk.*] You know what they're sayin'. You know what they were like. We've got things calmed down now—but you faced the mob when you got off the train at Galway.

PARNELL. [*Looks at DAVITT.*] Mob? They were very mild.

DAVITT. But before you came they had sticks and stones —an' they meant to use 'em. They let out such a roar when they saw you there—quiet—an' smilin'—I thought they meant to kill you. But thank God they were

cheerin'. But it can't be done again. I've come here in
love and loyalty to tell you, *It can't be done again*. It's not
just the voters. It's the boys at headquarters. Oh, Mr.
Parnell—for the sake of the Party—for the sake of Ireland. I tell you the bridge will not stand another load.

PARNELL. Michael, Home Rule is here. Today Mr. Gladstone told me he would move the first reading of the
bill this session.

DAVITT. Thank God.

PARNELL. Mrs. O'Shea carries my views to Gladstone
and his to me. Neither of us would have trusted them to
paper. Now he is arranging a house party at Hawarden
to celebrate our agreement. Mrs. O'Shea and her aunt
Mrs. Wood.

DAVITT. Mr. Parnell, I have no more to say. [*There is
a knock at the door.*] Come in.

MONTY. [*He enters—closes door behind him.*] Mr. Parnell, Captain O'Shea is here.

MICHAEL. I'll be goin'.

PARNELL. We'd be glad to have you stay, Michael.

DAVITT. I'll not be after seein' the Captain, thank you.
Will it be amiss if I slip out through the garden?

PARNELL. Certainly, if you like. Ask Captain O'Shea
to come in.

MONTY. Yes, sir. [*He exits—closing door.*]

PARNELL. Michael, have I ever broken my word?

DAVITT. Never.

PARNELL. I give you my word I shall never exert again a finger-weight of influence for Captain O'Shea.

DAVITT. *God* be praised—Mr. Parnell, if ye take a word from me—just don't scotch the snake. Kill it. It'll bite.

PARNELL. If it has time. Galway will keep him quiet for a while. Goodbye, Michael. Thank you.

DAVITT. God keep you. [DAVITT *exits.*]

O'SHEA. [*Enters.*] Hello, Parnell.

PARNELL. How do you do, O'Shea.

O'SHEA. Thought I'd never get here. Rotten train service. I can't afford the luxurious modes of travel of the Party chief. Where's Katie?

PARNELL. Why?

O'SHEA. I think it's urgent she hear what I have to say.

PARNELL. Very well. [*He rises and crosses to Upper Left door.*]

O'SHEA. [*Crossing to Left Center chair.*] I hear you are stabling your horses in the village.

PARNELL. Some of them. [*Calls.*] Katie, Willie's here. He wants to talk to us.

KATIE. Very well.

O'SHEA. Well, we turned the trick in Galway, didn't we?

PARNELL. [*Crossing back to front of desk.*] Yes, but it was far from easy.

O'SHEA. Oh, I knew you could manage it. [KATIE *enters Up Left.*] Hello, Katie.

KATIE. [*Taking a few steps into the room.*] Good afternoon, Willie.

PARNELL. [*Against desk.*] You're not very popular, Willie. Can't you try to get yourself liked a little more.

O'SHEA. I should be sorry if I were popular with the rapscallion crew you call "The Party."

PARNELL. [*Slightly humorous.*] I think you need never be sorry then.

O'SHEA. Oh, I'm popular enough except with your crowd.

PARNELL. Is that what you came here to tell me?

O'SHEA. I've a right to come here.

PARNELL. When Katie invites you.

O'SHEA. [*Nastily.*] It's to be inferred that she has invited you.

KATIE. [*Still Up Left Center. Quietly.*] Yes—and so have you, [*Crosses to desk Down Right.*] Wil'ie. Many times—and by letter.

O'SHEA. You're not very civil—either of you.

PARNELL. You started the subject, I believe. [KATIE *sits.*] I merely asked you why you had come?

O'SHEA. [*Turns chair.*] I came here because I'm not satisfied with the way I'm being treated.

PARNELL. Indeed.

O'SHEA. [*Sits.*] My services are invaluable to the Irish Party but what do I get in return?

PARNELL. Well—you've just been given Galway.

O'SHEA. Yes—the great privilege of a seat in the House of Commons.

KATIE. Willie—how can you?

PARNELL. You seemed very eager for that privilege at the last election.

O'SHEA. So I suppose you think I've come here to render thanks?

PARNELL. No. I never thought that for a moment.

O'SHEA. Well, you're quite right. I'm here because I want recognition.

PARNELL. Of what?

O'SHEA. Of my importance to the Party. And I want a suitable reward.

KATIE. You've just been elected from Galway.

O'SHEA. [*Scornfully.*] Galway!

PARNELL. Not quite suitable?

O'SHEA. Is that all I'm to get. Look here, I've kept my

temper pretty well up to now, but I won't be put off. I intend to demand my rights.

PARNELL. Your rights. What do you want?

O'SHEA. *Chief* Secretary for Ireland.

KATIE. [*Terrified.*] Willie.

O'SHEA. Parnell, if you don't tell your Party that you are under such obligations to me—

KATIE. Willie—are you mad?

O'SHEA. Such political obligations then—

PARNELL. It's no use, Willie.

O'SHEA. No use—let me tell you I could have got as much in another direction.

KATIE. [*Rises—then.*[What do you mean?

O'SHEA. Exactly what I say. But I've stuck to my bargain, haven't I? I always stick to a bargain—as long as I am paid.

PARNELL. [*Rises.*] My God, you've been paid.

O'SHEA. Do you think so? Well, if the Irish Party doesn't appreciate me—

PARNELL. [*Crosses Center.*] What have you on them? You've never even taken the Party oath.

O'SHEA. I shall vote as I please.

PARNELL. You won't even sit with them.

O'SHEA. I can't be made to sit even.

PARNELL. You mock and jeer them. [*Slowly.*] God himself couldn't make you Secretary for Ireland. [*Flick of second.*]

O'SHEA. But you could.

PARNELL. I can do no more.

O'SHEA. You mean you won't.

PARNELL. I couldn't— [*Turns, crosses up.*] if I would. [*Crosses back to desk.*]

O'SHEA. Couldn't you? [*Rises.*] Don't you think you'd better try?

KATIE. Willie—listen—be reasonable. You've just been given Galway. Wait. It takes time to arrange things of this sort.

O'SHEA. I happen to know the post is to be filled this week. [*Satirically.*] Perhaps you hadn't heard.

KATIE. If you will give us time—

O'SHEA. Mr. Parnell, have you anything further to say?

PARNELL. No.

[KATIE *turns to* PARNELL.]

O'SHEA. Too bad. Katie, I fear your influence isn't as potent as it was. Endearing young charms do fade.

PARNELL. [*Finally.*] O'Shea—get out.

O'SHEA. [*Crossing to door.*] Very well—good afternoon.

KATIE. Willie, don't go like that.

O'SHEA. [*At door.*] The old address will always find me, Katie. [*To* PARNELL.] You won't reconsider?

PARNELL. No.

O'SHEA. I think you're making a mistake.

PARNELL. Inevitably.

O'SHEA. Au revoir. [O'SHEA. *exits.* KATIE *sits.*]

KATIE. What did he mean when he said he could have got as much in another direction?

PARNELL. I don't know.

KATIE. I'm afraid. Can't you do something for him?

PARNELL. I'll see him in hell first.

KATIE. We've got to do something to keep him quiet.

PARNELL. Katie, my hands are tied. I'm powerless. The Party won't have him.

KATIE. But suppose—

PARNELL. There's nothing I can do.

KATIE. [*To him.*] Charles, you said Gladstone was waiting for his ace of trumps. For God's sake don't let him use Willie. Can't you make Gladstone bring in the bill sooner? Now—at once?

PARNELL. No.

KATIE. Think. There must be some way—

PARNELL. No.

KATIE. But we can't just—*wait*—

PARNELL. Perhaps, if I could— [*He breaks off.*]

KATIE. What?

PARNELL. I might write him—but it wouldn't do any good.

KATIE. What would you say—

PARNELL. I would ask him—but—he's not to be hurried.

KATIE. You can try—

PARNELL. Very well.

KATIE. I'll get paper— [*Crosses to Down Right desk. She seizes a pencil and paper and sits looking at him expectantly.*]

PARNELL. [*In Left Center chair. Dictates, and she writes.*] "My dear Mr. Gladstone,
    After the sweeping victory of the Irish Party in the recent elections it would seem that we were in for a time of peace and quiet. However, [*Rises and crosses to her.*] I find the temper of the people to be exactly the opposite. You will perhaps pardon me if I suggest to you"—it won't do any good, Katie. [*He stops.*]

KATIE. [*Looking up.*] Go on. Go on. [*Taking hand.*] I suggest—

PARNELL. [*Dictating.*] "—if I suggest that the *immedi-*

ate introduction of the Home Rule Bill, might have a calming effect, not only on members of the Irish Party but upon the people as a whole—"

[*During these lines the curtain falls.*]

CURTAIN

ACT TWO

Scene II

Scene—*The drawing room at Eltham.*
WILLIE O'SHEA *alone. His nerves are at tension. He paces up and down. Pauses at the table, opens a book, puts it down again. Walks to the fire and is standing with his back to the room when the door opens and* AUNT BEN *enters. He whirls around, startled.*

O'SHEA. Aunt Ben!

AUNT BEN. [*Crossing to chair and sits.*] You didn't expect to see me, did you, Willie?

O'SHEA. Well—I did—rather.

AUNT BEN. You tried to hope against hope.

O'SHEA. [*Slightly sullen.*] I came to see Katie of course.

AUNT BEN. You'll see her. Have you rung for whisky?

O'SHEA. There's some on the table, thanks. [*Crosses to table.*] I own I could do with a spot. [*Pours one for himself.*]

AUNT BEN. [*Slowly—as she crosses.*] I could myself. These last few days have not been easy. Thank you.

O'SHEA. [*Starts to pour her one. Starting to pour from the decanter.*] There. May I?

AUNT BEN. No. I'll compromise on a brandy. [*He pours hers and crosses to her with both glasses.*] Thank you.

O'SHEA. [*Definitely.*] Aunt Ben, is there any truth in this rumor that Katie means to fight the divorce?

AUNT BEN. Why shouldn't she?

O'SHEA. Why she can't. She hasn't a leg to stand on.

AUNT BEN. Really?

O'SHEA. She's begged for a divorce often enough.

AUNT BEN. But you wouldn't give it to her. Now—she has changed her mind.

O'SHEA. Much good that will do her. Everybody knows her relations with Parnell.

AUNT BEN. Quite so. *Everybody.* [*Puts glass down.*]

O'SHEA. Look here, Aunt Ben, if you're shooting at me I won't stand it—even from you. My honor has been tarnished—

AUNT BEN. The only person who has tarnished your honor, Willie, is yourself.

O'SHEA. I think you'll regret your attitude to me, Aunt Ben.

AUNT BEN. Well—if I don't have any more than that to regret—the Lord is kind.

O'SHEA. May I see Katie?

AUNT BEN. She will be down in a minute. What made you think she would defend the case, Willie?

O'SHEA. My solicitor got wind of it. He said she was naming Annie co-respondent.

AUNT BEN. Has Annie heard this too?

O'SHEA. Yes, I told her.

AUNT BEN. Dear! Dear! You're braver than I thought you were, Willie. [WILLIE *turns away impatiently. He has a vivid recollection of his interview with* ANNIE.] How did she take it?

O'SHEA. She wasn't exactly pleased.

AUNT BEN. So far Annie has always been able to eat her cake and have it too.

O'SHEA. The thing is impossible. Katie can't accuse her own sister of adultery. It's simply not done.

AUNT BEN. There's nothing like establishing a precedent. Just why did you bring suit for divorce?

O'SHEA. Why does any man? The usual reasons.

AUNT BEN. I express myself badly. I mean, why did you choose this particular moment to become aware of the usual reasons.

O'SHEA. Aunt Ben, I simply cannot allow you to insinuate—

AUNT BEN. Why not call a spade a spade. I thought you'd be glad to talk sense. You naturally want to do what's best—for yourself. Perhaps we might come to an agreement after all. The highest bidder usually wins, doesn't he?

[*The door is opened by* PHYLLIS.]

PHYLLIS. Mrs. Steele and Miss Wood, Ma'am.

[ANNIE *and* CLARA *come in.* ANNIE *sweeps by* O'SHEA *with a bare look and goes up to* AUNT BEN *and kisses her.*]

O'SHEA. Annie!

ANNIE. Aunt Ben.

AUNT BEN. How do you do, Annie? Phyllis, will you ask Mrs. O'Shea to come down?

PHYLLIS. Yes, Ma'am.

AUNT BEN. I thought we would be seeing you. I did not foresee Clara, however.

CLARA. I thought under the circumstances dear Annie needed—

AUNT BEN. [*Drily.*] A sister's love. Quite so. Very prudent of you, Annie. I *should* have foreseen Clara. [ANNIE *crosses up to Right back window.*] Well, Clara, has Thomas' Hotel been as respectable as you feared.

CLARA. Aunt Ben. [*She flutters over to* WILLIE.] How do you do, Willie?

O'SHEA. Rotten, thanks.

AUNT BEN. Quite a family gathering. Do lay aside your wraps.

ANNIE. No thank you, Aunt Ben. [*Crosses up to Right back window.*]

CLARA. We can't stay long.

AUNT BEN. Annie, did you give orders to have them feed and water your horses?

ANNIE. I sent the carriage to the Inn in the village.

AUNT BEN. As you please, but Mr. Parnell tells me the grooms there are exceedingly careless.

[*At the mention of* PARNELL'S *name, they look at each other and away. The door opens and* KATIE *comes in. She closes the door keeping her face to the room and for a moment she gives the impression of standing with her back to the wall. Slowly closes door.*]

KATIE. [*At right door.*] How do you do—everybody? [*A pause.*] Well—who'll begin? I suppose you don't want to waste time inquiring how I am—or discussing the weather.

ANNIE. [*Rages.*] Not in the least. I'll begin. Yesterday, Willie, came to me with some cock and bull story that my name was to be dragged into this disgraceful mess you've got yourself into. I couldn't believe it but I decided to come down and find out. Is it true?

CLARA. I cannot believe it.

[AUNT BEN *looks at* CLARA *and she relapses into silence.*]

O'SHEA. Annie, I suggest that you let me talk to Katie first.

ANNIE. [*Shutting him up.*] You've done enough talking, I think.

O'SHEA. If you'll let me see her—alone—that's what I came down here for—

ANNIE. I tell you, you and Katie have talked enough. Between you you are starting a hideous scandal—and I am the victim.

O'SHEA. If you'll only let me see her alone I can arrange things. I can manage her.

KATIE. You always have—haven't you, Willie?

O'SHEA. Katie, you surely can't mean to bring Annie into this. You wouldn't—your own sister.

ANNIE. [*To* KATIE.] My name has never been dragged in the mud.

AUNT BEN. You've been very lucky, Annie.

ANNIE. [*To* AUNT BEN.] What do you mean?

AUNT BEN. "Lucky?" Means favored by chance.

ANNIE. The fact remains, however, my name has not been bandied about in the public prints.

O'SHEA. What about *my* name?

ANNIE. [*No assistance.*] Willie, for once forget yourself and think of somebody else.

AUNT BEN. Don't ask the impossible, Annie.

ANNIE. [*She has shut him up. Crosses toward* KATIE. *Deliberately. To* KATIE.] I have come here to find out the truth. Are you going to drag me into this?

CLARA. Katie—you wouldn't—you couldn't—remember who you are—think—

ANNIE. Is it true?

CLARA. [*Desperately, a squealing mouse.*] I'm *sure* it isn't.

KATIE. It is perfectly true.

ANNIE. [*Crosses closer to* KATIE.] Well—I won't have it. I won't be treated in this way. What have I ever done to you. When I heard the talk about you and Parnell— what did I do? Invited you to the opera.

CLARA. But, Annie, Mr. Parnell wouldn't go.

ANNIE. [*Turns to her.*] Shut up! Be quiet. [*Crosses to* KATIE.] I didn't care. I was glad you were amusing your-self. It seemed more normal. You could have had an affair with a crossing sweeper and I would have—

KATIE. Invited him to the opera?

ANNIE. [*Turns and crosses toward* KATIE.] I won't be treated this way. You haven't the slightest shred of evidence against me—

O'SHEA. You've absolutely nothing to go on—you can't prove a thing—

KATIE. [*To* ANNIE.] Willie is your lover. Can you deny it? [ANNIE *crosses Up Center.*] You don't suppose I *want* to prove it—but I can. Unless Willie withdraws this suit—I shall.

CLARA. I never would have believed it.

AUNT BEN. Oh, wouldn't you, Clara?

CLARA. [*With injured dignity.*] I mean that Katie would do such a thing. I am shocked beyond words. [*Crosses Center. To* KATIE.] If you care anything for the family name—if you have the slightest consideration for—

KATIE. I care nothing for the family name—or for your name, Annie—or for my own. Nothing at all.

ANNIE [*Crosses behind sofa. Stares at* KATIE *for a second. There is something here she is curious to understand. Then she turns to* WILLIE.] You got me into this —now, you can get me out.

O'SHEA. What can I do?

ANNIE. You can withdraw your suit.

O'SHEA. Annie—I—I can't.

ANNIE. *Can't?*

O'SHEA. It's impossible. You don't understand.

ANNIE. [*Crosses behind him.*] Oh, yes I do. Quite. You kept silent as long as it suited you. Now it doesn't, God knows why—

AUNT BEN. It isn't necessary to invoke the Deity, Annie, to discover Willie's reasons.

ANNIE. And you've decided to talk. You never dreamed Katie would talk back. You think now you can manage her because you always have. You're wrong. Katie has her back to the wall and Aunt Ben is beside her. Maybe you think you can fight Aunt Ben.

AUNT BEN. Oh!

ANNIE. You haven't known her as long as I have. Take my advice, Willie, get out of this and get out now.

O'SHEA. She's only trying to blacken us to save him. That's the size of it. But you can't do it, Katie. If you think you can explain away Parnell—

AUNT BEN. How did you manage it so cleverly, Willie?

KATIE. I have no intention of explaining away Parnell.

[CLARA *turns to* KATIE. ANNIE *looks at* KATIE.]

O'SHEA. What are you going to do then?

KATIE. I intend to explain *you,* Willie.

ANNIE. [*Crosses to* KATIE.] Do you mean you're not going to deny your relations with that man? Is that what you're saying?

KATIE. Just that.

ANNIE. You're a fool. You don't even play the game.

KATIE. I don't play your game, Annie.

ANNIE. Well, if you want to save your skin alive you'd better begin. I don't care in the least whom you flirt with —or sleep with—but for God's sake don't shriek it aloud in Piccadilly Circus.

CLARA. This is becoming too painful. Can't someone stop it. [*Crosses Up Center.*]

KATIE. Yes, Willie O'Shea. I tell you *I* can't.

ANNIE. Katie—I'm warning you—

AUNT BEN. Annie, Annie, don't you think the best thing for you to do is to return home and let me talk to Willie?

CLARA. You'd better talk to Katie too, while you're about it.

AUNT BEN. [*To* ANNIE.] And take Clara with you.

ANNIE. [*Crosses toward* AUNT BEN.] Yes, I shall go. Katie has lost her senses. Perhaps if we give her time she may get some of them back. [*With a withering look at* WILLIE.] Aunt Ben, if you have any influence over either of them make them drop this. [*To* KATIE—*crosses Right Center.*] If there is any public washing of dirty linen—you will be sorry to your dying day.

KATIE. [*Slowly.*] If there is a public washing— [*She breaks off.*] I shall be sorry to my dying day.

ANNIE. Come Clara. [WILLIE *crosses to open the door for them. Crossing Right door.*] Goodbye, Aunt Ben.

[ANNIE *exits.*]

CLARA. [*Tearfully. Crosses up to* AUNT BEN.] Goodbye, Aunt Ben.

AUNT BEN. Goodbye, Clara.

CLARA. [*Going.*] The innocent always suffer with the guilty.

AUNT BEN. A little vicarious suffering won't hurt you, Clara. [ANNIE *sweeps out.* CLARA *follows her.* WILLIE *closes the door.*] You'd better give it up, Willie.

KATIE. Now that you know Annie's name will be brought in, surely you won't go on.

O'SHEA. [*Crosses to* KATIE.] You're afraid if this scandal breaks Parnell will be ruined. You're quite right. He will. You're only using Annie to frighten me off.

KATIE. [*Crosses close to him.*] Willie for years I have begged you to let me go—to divorce me. Now, I beg you, I implore you—not to.

O'SHEA. I intend to divorce you.

AUNT BEN. [*Sharply.*] Katie, let me talk to him. Better give it up, Willie.

O'SHEA. [*Turns and steps to her.*] Aunt Ben, you're a wonderful woman. You should have been a man. By George you'd have cracked the whip and given 'em hell.

AUNT BEN. I can crack a pretty good whip as it is, Willie.

O'SHEA. Only, I'm not afraid of it. You can't prove anything against me, and you can't prove anything against Annie. I know that well enough.

AUNT BEN. Legal proof *is* difficult.

O'SHEA. I think you'll find it so.

AUNT BEN. Merely a relative term, however.

O'SHEA. Well, whatever it is you have to have it in a court of law. Suspicion is one thing, proof is another.

AUNT BEN. How true. I suspected you and Annie long before I had proof.

O'SHEA. Had—proof?

AUNT BEN. Willie, you, and Annie, and I, have been guests at various country houses simultaneously. My maid, Morton—you remember her. She will make an excellent witness. [*Pauses.*] You'd better give it up, Willie.

O'SHEA. [*To* KATIE.] You're going to sacrifice your own sister to save *him*.

KATIE. Won't you ever understand. I will sacrifice anything to save him.

O'SHEA. You won't sacrifice me, I'll tell you that. I've never set myself up on a pedestal of leadership and virtue. I'm sorry for Annie, of course—

AUNT BEN. Somehow I didn't think Annie's sorrows would affect you—sufficiently. [*Rises.*] Your own sorrows are what I am really counting on. When you see yourself as all England will see you, the *mari complaisant,* the consenting husband—

O'SHEA. You'll never make out a case.

AUNT BEN. The willfully blind—

O'SHEA. I trusted her.

AUNT BEN. And profited by it.

O'SHEA. You can talk all you like. I trusted my wife and was deceived.

AUNT BEN. You never dreamed that Parnell was your wife's lover.

O'SHEA. No.

KATIE. Willie, how can you!

AUNT BEN. Even when London was agog.

O'SHEA. No!

AUNT BEN. And when the papers began to hint at the story, even then, you still—trusted.

O'SHEA. Yes.

KATIE. That's not the truth.

AUNT BEN. Katie, please—then why, after an article appeared in a London paper did you write a letter to Katie begging her to be more careful about being seen in public so much with Mr. Parnell.

O'SHEA. I didn't.

AUNT BEN. After that article appeared, you remember coming down here to see her?

O'SHEA. Yes.

AUNT BEN. But she was out—so you wrote a note—

O'SHEA. [*Involuntarily.*] I tore it up.

AUNT BEN. And threw it in the waste basket. Imprudent, Willie. Very. [O'SHEA *sits. He turns abruptly and stares into the fire.*] There's an easy way out, Willie. [*Slow talk here.*]

O'SHEA. [*Turning around.*] Easy!

AUNT BEN. Withdraw the suit.

O'SHEA. My God, do you think that's easy.

AUNT BEN. I will double your allowance. [O'SHEA *shakes his head.*] I will make you a substantial settlement. [O'SHEA *shakes his head with growing sadness.*] Ten thousand pounds.

O'SHEA. [*Rises.*] I can't.

AUNT BEN. Willie—on the day you withdraw your suit, I will give you twenty thousand pounds.

O'SHEA. [*Agonized.*] Oh, my God, Aunt Ben. Why didn't you come to me sooner.

KATIE. There's no use going on, Aunt Ben. I've sold out—and *not* to the highest bidder. I think you'd better go, Willie.

[O'SHEA *walks to the door.*]

KATIE. [*Strong voice—stops him.*] Willie, I'll stop at nothing—I will do anything—anything.

O'SHEA. Yes, so would I. The trouble is there isn't anything to do—now. [*He goes.*]

KATIE. He's going through with it. So am I. To get even a part of the truth known, I'd burn at the stake.

AUNT BEN. [*Warningly—looking at her.*] This will be worse than the stake if I know anything about English Divorce Courts. You might as well be stripped naked for the crowd to spit on.

KATIE. Aunt Ben, there is only one thing that matters to me at all. All other things—just aren't there.

AUNT BEN. Very well, my dear.

KATIE. But it will be awful for you. Oh, Aunt Ben— [*Crosses to* AUNT BEN—*kneels.*] don't—don't stay in England.

AUNT BEN. Katie—we've traveled a long road together since you used to bring me wilted daisies and wet kisses. We won't part now.

[*The door opens.* PARNELL *comes in.*]

PARNELL. [*At door.*] What was O'Shea doing here? I passed him on the drive.

[KATIE *rises.* AUNT BEN *rises.*]

AUNT BEN. I wanted to talk to him.

PARNELL. Was he disagreeable?

AUNT BEN. [*Crosses Center.*] Oh, no. I'll claim that prize. I tried to force him to withdraw his suit.

PARNELL. [*Tensely.*] And—is he going to?

AUNT BEN. [*Crossing to Right door.*] No. But I think I've convinced him that Katie's defense—

PARNELL. Katie's defense!

AUNT BEN. Yes, it will be something more than he bargained for. [AUNT BEN *exits.*]

PARNELL. [*With strength.*] You're not going to defend the suit Katie. [*Closes door—crosses to* KATIE—*they embrace.*]

KATIE. I didn't tell you till I was sure Willie meant to go on. I have engaged counsel.

PARNELL. [*Crosses to her.*] We are not going to defend the case, Katie.

KATIE. But we can *prove* that Willie knew— [*Slowly.*]

PARNELL. Many things. So many that O'Shea will never get his divorce. What do you gain by that?

KATIE. The truth. If people know the truth—oh, don't you see—you will not be blamed.

PARNELL. And you will still be the wife of Willie O'Shea.

KATIE. You can't mean that you're going to stand by and do nothing while Willie ruins your life out of spite.

PARNELL. I have decided.

KATIE. This is political suicide. You know that. You will be ruined.

PARNELL. There will be no defense.

KATIE. I won't consent. If you refuse to defend yourself—

PARNELL. [*Crosses after her.*] I shall not even employ counsel.

KATIE. [*Turns to him.*] I shall, I shall have the best counsel for the defense in London—I shall tell the truth—

PARNELL. And be tied to Willie O'Shea for the rest of your life.

KATIE. [*Sits.*] I have been for years—it will be no worse.

PARNELL. Won't it? Can you conceive the length he will go to when the world knows the black-mailing swine he is? Have you thought of the misery he'll put on you for your part in it? Willie coming to me for favors is one thing—Willie publicly branded malignant is another. Do you think I'll leave you to him? His physical property under the law? [*Tenderly. Crosses to her. Picks up her head.* SHE *cries on his shoulder.*] Darling, isn't a divorce what we always wanted? Now it's come—and you weep.

KATIE. Not this way—not now.

PARNELL. Nothing comes the way you want it, or when you want it, but if you want it—enough—you take it. [KATIE *is sobbing.*] My sweet, don't—don't cry. Just because O'Shea wins his divorce doesn't mean I'm ruined. There'll be some to stand by me.

KATIE. And will the Honorable William Ewart Gladstone be among them?

PARNELL. When the Party sticks by me, he will. He'll have to. He knows that well enough.

KATIE. And will the Party—stick?

PARNELL. I think so.

KATIE. Oh, my darling—I am afraid.

PARNELL. Katie, look at me. [*Pushes away her head.*] Don't be afraid. We have no regrets, no fears, no remorse. We don't know the future—but in this instant, this present, I have you. It is enough.

KATIE. [*He's persuaded her.*] Is it enough? The work you've given your life for— [*Her hands fall to her sides in an expressive gesture.*] Am I worth the bitterness of that?

PARNELL. Bitterness and sorrow are all no matter—because there is no one else in all the world that matters at all.

KATIE. The world—this brief moment—oh, my darling, so brief; and then—what? Shall I lose you?

PARNELL. No, in some other world—some other point in time—we shall be drawn together again by the sheer force of my longing for you.

CURTAIN

ACT THREE

ACT THREE

Scene I

SCENE—*The Prime Minister's study, Number 10 Downing Street. Large folding doors at the back which are closed. Left, door leading to the hall. Long windows, Right.* GLADSTONE *is seated at his desk writing. It is late afternoon in November, the lamps are already lighted. A young secretary, his name is* STANLEY, *opens the door from the anteroom and comes in. He crosses and stands by* GLADSTONE'S *side waiting to be noticed.*

GLADSTONE. [*Looking up after a moment.*] Yes, Mr. Stanley?

STANLEY. Mr. Timothy Healy is here, Sir, by appointment.

GLADSTONE. Yes, yes. Quite so. [*He carefully lays down his pen, wipes it, then looks up.*] Mr. Stanley, will you be good enough to listen carefully. I have a few simple instructions which I wish you to understand before you show in Mr. Healy.

STANLEY. Yes, Mr. Gladstone.

109

GLADSTONE. Thank you. Mr. Healy, I believe has the appointment for four o'clock?

STANLEY. Yes, Sir. It is four minutes before four, Sir, now, I think.

GLADSTONE. [*Looking at his watch.*] Two and a half. I have an appointment with Mrs. Wood and Mrs. O'Shea at a quarter past four?

STANLEY. Yes, Sir.

GLADSTONE. When they come they are to be shown into the library, not the anteroom, Mr. Stanley.

STANLEY. Yes, Sir.

GLADSTONE. And then, Mr. Stanley, as soon as they come, will you immediately let me know—

STANLEY. Interrupt you, Sir?

GLADSTONE. Exactly. Interrupt me and then, contrary to our usual custom if other callers are present, will you announce their names?

STANLEY. Yes, Sir.

GLADSTONE. And, Mr. Stanley will you be good enough to announce their names in audible tones?

STANLEY. Yes, Mr. Gladstone.

GLADSTONE. This too is contrary to custom, your usual tones, even when spoken in my ear, being quite inaudible.

STANLEY. Yes, Mr. Gladstone.

GLADSTONE. You are sure you understand?

STANLEY. Yes, Sir. When the ladies come I am to inform you of the fact in *audible* tones.

GLADSTONE. Very good. You may ask Mr. Healy to come in now.

STANLEY. Yes, Sir. [*He crosses, opens the door to the anteroom and we hear him say, just outside—softly.*] Mr. Gladstone will see you, Mr. Healy.

[HEALY *enters followed by the* SECRETARY, *who closes the door behind him, crosses and goes out through the double doors to the library.*]

GLADSTONE. [*Rises from his chair with hand outstretched. He is beaming genially though perhaps, for the sensitive, a shade too patronizing. The smiling blue grey eyes can turn to slate, and the smiling mouth to a hard, straight line.*] My dear Mr. Healy, [HEALY *crosses to* GLADSTONE *who shakes hands with him.*] how very good of you to come.

HEALY. [*Bowing awkwardly. Unfamiliar with this kind of thing.*] Prime Minister.

GLADSTONE. Will you smoke?

HEALY. Thank you, no, Sir.

GLADSTONE. Do sit down, Mr. Healy. [HEALY *sits.*] One can so often arrive [GLADSTONE *sits.*] at the solution of a problem if one can talk face to face.

HEALY. I can scarcely hope for such an outcome in the present instance, Sir.

GLADSTONE. Why not, Mr. Healy?

HEALY. Mr. Gladstone, you promised the Irish Party
that you would bring in the Home Rule Bill. You have
not done so. I do not see much room for argument in the
matter.

GLADSTONE. Whatever I may have promised, I promised
to Mr. Parnell.

HEALY. He *is* the Irish Party, Mr. Gladstone.

GLADSTONE. There, I am sorry, I cannot agree with you.
How is he? I heard he had been ill.

HEALY. Very ill. He has recovered, however.

GLADSTONE. I cannot tell you how much he has been in
my thoughts. Poor fellow, poor fellow. Have you seen
him since the divorce suit?

HEALY. He was at a meeting yesterday.

GLADSTONE. [*Solicitously.*] Ah—and how did he look?

HEALY. Well—to be exact—he looked as though we
were the ones who had committed the adultery.

GLADSTONE. [*His heavy pity slightly set back.*] Ah—a
dominant personality—an unbending will. [*Comes forward.*] You will pardon me if I say that I have sometimes wondered how a man of your keen mind, and
strength of character, could at all times submit yourself
to the complete dominance of even a Parnell.

HEALY. I am proud to serve under him.

GLADSTONE. Ah—you are very modest, Mr. Healy, exceedingly modest. Parnell *is* wonderful of course. What a tragedy! Poor fellow, what a fall!

HEALY. I was not aware of any fall, Sir. Parnell is still Leader of the Irish Party.

GLADSTONE. His continued leadership, Mr. Healy, would be fatal to the Irish cause.

HEALY. I do not agree with you, Sir.

GLADSTONE. His usefulness is at an end.

HEALY. [*No answer.*] Why should a man's private life affect his public career?

GLADSTONE. I cannot tell you, Mr. Healy. I only know that it does. Do not think me antagonistic—unsympathetic—

HEALY. I cannot reconcile your sympathetic thoughts with your actions, Mr. Gladstone. You have issued a public letter, printed in the newspapers, in which you say that unless Parnell resigns you will feel called upon to do so.

GLADSTONE. [*Smiling quietly.*] Did I say I would resign, Mr. Healy?

HEALY. You said—well—everyone took it to mean that. What did you mean, Mr. Gladstone?

GLADSTONE. I think I cannot usefully add to what I have already written. Consider for a moment, my position in this matter.

HEALY. I have no doubt you have fully considered it, Sir.

GLADSTONE. I am not only the Leader of the Liberal Party, but I am the unofficial leader of the Non-Conformist Church Party. Suddenly I find myself hand in glove with the chief figure in a hideous divorce scandal. What can I do? I assure you these people view the matter entirely from the moral point of view. The pressure brought to bear on me has been enormous. I must heed their voice.

HEALY. Must you? Why, Mr. Gladstone?

GLADSTONE. Perhaps because it is the most shrill.

HEALY. You will pardon me if I suggest that the voice which swept you to Number Ten Downing Street, might be worth heeding.

GLADSTONE. [*Raising a deprecating hand.*] I am not unmindful of the Irish vote, nor the Irish cause. But this question goes beyond the political. I beg you to consider it from the moral aspect.

HEALY. Mr. Gladstone, the Irish are fighting a political war. What would you think of soldiers who stopped in the midst of battle to inquire whether or not their general had broken one of the Ten Commandments?

GLADSTONE. [*With a slight tightening of the lips—a repressed smile.*] I should immediately surmise that they were of the Non-Conformist Group.

HEALY. But we are not. If you have decided to break with us—

GLADSTONE. Mr. Healy, you wrong me. Such a thing was furthest from my thoughts. My manifesto was directed solely against Charles Parnell, not the Irish Party.

HEALY. [*Conversationally.*] He *is* the Irish Party.

GLADSTONE. Again I am impressed with your modesty, Mr. Healy.

HEALY. Because he has gone wrong in a private question is that a reason why he should fail in his duty to his people?

GLADSTONE. [*In a ringing voice.*] He would not fail. Others will fail him.

HEALY. [*Fighting back.*] We shall not. I'm sure of that.

GLADSTONE. [*Strong. Deadly definite. His eyes piercing steel.*] Are you—Mr. Healy—*Sure?* The leader of the Irish Party is enveloped in the nauseous fumes of the divorce court. They rise to Heaven, and yet you persist in a policy which bids fair to wreck your Party. Is Mr. Parnell the only Irishman capable of leading you? Are the forceful, brilliant men of your Party a lot of weaklings? No, Mr. Healy, I am impressed with your modesty but I find it deplorable.

HEALY. [*Less certainly, more pleadingly.*] He has led us forth out of the wilderness. We are within sight of the Promised Land—

GLADSTONE. Call upon your knowledge of Scripture further, Mr. Healy. Remember, Moses was allowed to see but not to enter the Promised Land.

[*The folding doors open and* STANLEY *enters and pauses.*]

GLADSTONE. Yes, Mr. Stanley?

STANLEY. I beg your pardon, Mr. Gladstone. Mrs. Wood and Mrs. O'Shea. [*Looks out.*]

GLADSTONE. [*Watching* HEALY.] Ask them to be seated. I shall be with them shortly.

STANLEY. Yes, Sir. [*He goes, closing the double doors after him.*]

HEALY. [*Rises as does* GLADSTONE.] I will bid you good afternoon, Mr. Gladstone.

GLADSTONE. I have a following appointment. No doubt you heard the names of my callers.

HEALY. Yes, Mr. Gladstone.

GLADSTONE. [*Persuasively.*] God knows how I regret being the instrument chosen for the downfall of such a man. But I cannot be entirely wrong in my estimate of the mettle of the Irish Party. I cannot but feel that the Irish cause is greater than the fall of one man. Do you not agree with me, Mr. Healy?

HEALY. I do not know, Mr. Gladstone.

GLADSTONE. Ah—you too wish only to do what is wisest and best. There is a hope in my heart that there shall arise some day a new and greater leader. One with whom I could join hands. Ah, what could we not do for Ireland. I shall pray to that end. [*Planted—firm—brusque.*

Holding out his hand.] You were good to come to me, Mr. Healy. I thank you.

HEALY. I am most sensible of the honor and most grateful. Good afternoon. [*He bows and goes out through the anteroom.*]

[GLADSTONE *walks to his table desk and rings a bell. The* SECRETARY *opens the double doors and comes into the room.*]

GLADSTONE. [*With a beaming smile, a mellow, warming smile.*] Ask Mrs. Wood and Mrs. O'Shea to come in.

[STANLEY *goes into the library and in a moment* AUNT BEN *and* KATIE *come in.* STANLEY *enters.*]

STANLEY. Mrs. Wood and Mrs. O'Shea, Sir.

GLADSTONE. [*Hand outstretched to* AUNT BEN.] My dear old friend.

AUNT BEN. [*Shaking hands.*] Prime Minister.

GLADSTONE. [*Crosses to her.*] And Mrs. O'Shea. I'm glad to see you again after all these months. [*Shakes hands with* KATIE *too.*] I am indeed glad to see you. [*To Right chair.*] Will you sit here, Caroline? [*To chair before desk, pulls back.*] And Mrs. O'Shea?

STANLEY. Shall you need me further, Sir?

GLADSTONE. Anyone else waiting?

STANLEY. Only Morrison of the Foreign Office.

GLADSTONE. Ask him to leave a message with you, or if he prefers, I shall see him tomorrow.

STANLEY. Yes, Sir. [*He goes into the anteroom.*]

AUNT BEN. You are looking very well, Prime Minister.

[KATIE *sits quietly, her eyes fixed on* GLADSTONE *most of the time.*]

GLADSTONE. [*Sitting.*] Thanks to a Fatherly Providence and my own simple habits of life, I am in most excellent condition.

AUNT BEN. I congratulate you. Providence never seemed to take the least interest in my health, perhaps because I never practised the simple life.

GLADSTONE. Ah, you know where that leads.

AUNT BEN. To gout.

GLADSTONE. And restlessness of soul.

AUNT BEN. But I always did have a restless soul.

GLADSTONE. Yes, Caroline, you did.

AUNT BEN. But, William, it doesn't junket about nearly as much as it used to. [GLADSTONE *smiles back. For the moment he is quite human.*] Well, enough of me.— May I broach a more important subject?

GLADSTONE. There is nothing more important than consideration of the human soul.

AUNT BEN. But it does take time—to really cover the subject?

KATIE. Mr. Gladstone—we have come to talk to you about Mr. Parnell.

GLADSTONE. Yes, Mrs. O'Shea.

KATIE. Why have you turned against him?

GLADSTONE. "Turned against him?" Surely that is too strong a statement.

KATIE. Is it? I hope so.

GLADSTONE. I differ from Mr. Parnell on a question of political expedience.

KATIE. You insist that he resign. Why?

GLADSTONE. Because I think it best for the Irish Party.

KATIE. If you destroy him you destroy the *Irish Party*. Is that what you want to do?

GLADSTONE. Mrs. O'Shea, I can only repeat that I feel that Mr. Parnell's political usefulness is at an end.

KATIE. Why?

GLADSTONE. Need we go into that?

KATIE. Is he less able to lead his people?

GLADSTONE. He is not only less able—he is unable.

KATIE. Why?

GLADSTONE. Because he will be repudiated.

KATIE. No—no, he will not. They won't fail him. I know it.

GLADSTONE. Are you sure?

KATIE. Absolutely.

GLADSTONE. Then why do you come to me?

KATIE. [*He has struck her.*] You're right. I am not sure. I was until you turned against him. There was no question of his leadership until then. I have hurt him—but it is you who are hurting him now. Is he less skillful, less adroit, less devoted?

GLADSTONE. Mr. Parnell has deviated from the accepted code. This deviation has become public property.

KATIE. That's it, isn't it? The accepted code is "Thou shalt not be found out," because everyone knows that I'm his mistress.

GLADSTONE. [*Shocked.*] Mrs. O'Shea!

KATIE. I am not his wife, Mr. Gladstone, what term shall I use?

GLADSTONE. My dear young lady—I entreat you—

KATIE. I beg your pardon. Because Mr. Parnell has figured in a divorce scandal—

GLADSTONE. Which has rocked London. Therefore he is disqualified from further public leadership.

KATIE. [*At* GLADSTONE.] You are cruel.

GLADSTONE. In your sorrow, Mrs. O'Shea, you are unjust. But it is natural, I forgive you. My heart bleeds for you but I must refuse to consider the fate of one man when weighed against the fate of a nation. My supreme duty is to Ireland.

KATIE. Is your heart really devoted to Ireland?

GLADSTONE. Have I not said so?

KATIE. And for the sake of Ireland you feel that Mr. Parnell must resign?

GLADSTONE. [*Feelingly.*] For the sake of Ireland.

KATIE. He will resign, Mr. Gladstone.

GLADSTONE. He will— Are you *assured* of this, Mrs. O'Shea?

KATIE. Quite. He will resign immediately, if you will give him your word that you will continue to support the Home Rule Bill.

[*There is a long pause, broken by* AUNT BEN.]

AUNT BEN. Well, William. Two birds with one stone. Could you possibly miss a chance like that?

KATIE. We have come to your terms.

GLADSTONE. I made no terms.

AUNT BEN. You demanded Parnell's resignation.

GLADSTONE. This is a very grave matter. I cannot possibly answer you now. I must take time to consider.

KATIE. The Irish Party meets tonight; there is no time.

GLADSTONE. It is my custom to give all questions my most serious consideration and prayerful thought.

AUNT BEN. Prime Minister, do you expect the Irish Party to wait till you finish praying.

GLADSTONE. [*Sternly.*] Caroline, I expect nothing of the Irish Party. They must act as they see fit.

KATIE. But, if Mr. Parnell resigns what further questions can there be?

GLADSTONE. You seem to overlook one factor in this case and the most important.

KATIE. What is it?

GLADSTONE. The moral issue.

KATIE. What moral question is involved in your support of the Home Rule Bill, Mr. Gladstone?

GLADSTONE. [*Very specifically.*] The question of how far one is justified, even for a great cause, in dealing with one who has defied the law of God and man. The evil of our time is the loss of the sense of sin. Shall I be condoning sin?

AUNT BEN. You condoned it as long as it was useful to you.

GLADSTONE. [*Indignantly.*] You cannot mean that I was aware of the private life of Mr. Parnell.

KATIE. [*Very pinningly.*] Were you not? You are a man of the world as well as a Churchman. When you could not find Mr. Parnell in the House or at his rooms you called on me. You are not a priest or a monk. What did you think? You must have known—the whole Government must have known.

AUNT BEN. Not officially, my dear. Governments, especially Liberal Governments are simple-minded and of childlike innocence.

KATIE. Once you asked me what my interest was in politics, I said "Entirely a personal one." You smiled. For a moment I thought—

GLADSTONE. You surely did not think I knew.

KATIE. [*It's not wise to keep this up.*] Only for a moment.

AUNT BEN. [*Starts a temper. Seething.*] It was a matter of common gossip.

GLADSTONE. I do not listen to the gossip of the lobbies.

AUNT BEN. Nor to the reports of the Secret Service? Mr. Parnell has been under surveillance for years.

GLADSTONE. Can you prove that, Mrs. Wood?

AUNT BEN. [*Madder.*] Probably not, if you take steps to prevent it, but I know it to be true. I also know that this situation was discussed by your Cabinet months ago. Parnell's help was indispensable. But should this scandal break, could you succeed in wiggling out with a whole tail left to your coat? You decided you could and you were probably right. I can't prove that either.

[GLADSTONE *raps on table. He rises.*]

KATIE. [*Alarmed.*] Aunt Ben—don't. [*Rises.*] We didn't come here for this, but to plead with you. [GLADSTONE *half turns away.*] Surely if Mr. Parnell resigns you will not be criticized. Mr. Gladstone— [*She sits.*] he could have saved himself politically if he had defended the divorce. But I would have been left tied to a man I loathed and feared. It was to save me—

GLADSTONE. Mrs. O'Shea, please—I do not doubt for an instant Parnell's personal honour or that he kept silent on many things—

AUNT BEN. Yes—for instance that Captain O'Shea should bring his suit at this particular time, this particular political situation. Shall I tell you why?

GLADSTONE. I fail to see the purpose—

AUNT BEN. And—at the moment—Captain O'Shea's income is strangely adequate. Would you like to know the why of that too?

GLADSTONE. [*Definite. Sharply to* KATIE.] I think we shall have something to regret if your aunt continues.

KATIE. Oh, Aunt Ben—please—please—Mr. Gladstone, forgive anything unwise we may have said. Don't let it count against— [*Her voice breaks.*]

AUNT BEN. [*Rises and crosses to* KATIE.] My dear, you are overwrought. [GLADSTONE *rises.*] We must go home. Come. We have done all we could.

GLADSTONE. [*Crosses to door.*] Yes. Your aunt is right. You should go home and rest.

KATIE. And what of the offer I have brought you to-night from Mr. Parnell?

GLADSTONE I shall give it due consideration—but of course I should have to have such a proposal in writing.

There is scarcely time for that before the meeting to-night.

KATIE. [*Rises.*] I have brought you many important proposals before this—*not* in writing.

GLADSTONE. But never in so grave a crisis.

KATIE. Mr. Gladstone, Mr. Parnell has already arranged that a committee from the Party bring you his proposals tonight.

GLADSTONE. I am very sorry but— [GLADSTONE *opens door.*]

AUNT BEN. [*After a look at* KATIE.] Prime Minister—good evening. [AUNT BEN *exits.*]

KATIE. Good night, Mr. Gladstone. [*With a gasping little sob.*] I beg you— I beg you.

GLADSTONE. My dear, good night.

KATIE. No, please listen to me. We'll go away—out of England. He couldn't harm you then. Your name will be quite safe. We will be forgotten.

GLADSTONE. Do you think so? Good night, Mrs. O'Shea.

[KATIE *exits.* GLADSTONE *closes door, crosses to desk and rings bell. Count of five.* STANLEY *enters.*]

STANLEY. I couldn't interrupt you—but Mr. Healy is back with Mr. Redmond.

GLADSTONE. [*Sternly and curtly.*] Their business?

STANLEY. They said they were straight from Mr. Parnell. That you would understand.

GLADSTONE. [*He's broken the Party.*] I do quite. [*Turns to him.*] Mr. Stanley, will you give orders to have a supper tray brought to me here at once. Something light. I shall not dine.

STANLEY. [*Turns.*] Yes, Sir. But—Mr. Healy and Mr. Redmond? What shall I tell them?

GLADSTONE. To wait, Mr. Stanley—to *wait*. Offer them tea—whisky if they prefer. Ask the gentlemen to *wait*.

[*He sits.*]

STANLEY. Yes, Sir. [STANLEY *is moving to the anteroom door and* GLADSTONE *has seated himself at his desk and is making little drawings, quite absorbed in his thoughts, as the curtain falls.*]

CURTAIN

ACT THREE

Scene II

SCENE—*Committee Room Number 15 in the House of Commons. Evening. The room is lit by candles.*
MURPHY *is arranging chairs about a center table.* MICHAEL DAVITT *subdued and sad comes in—anxious.*
*Tension—*MURPHY *feels all will be well as soon as* PARNELL *arrives.*

MURPHY. [*Pushing chair in—places it.*] Evenin' Mr. Davitt.

DAVITT. Mr. Healy got back yet?

MURPHY. [*Putting in 2nd chair.*] No, Sir. Neither Mr. Healy nor Mr. Redmond.

DAVITT. [*Sits.*] They're a long time.

MURPHY. Well I don't suppose a talk with the Prime Minister is easy come by. They likely had to wait. Mr. Parnell's here, Sir.

DAVITT. Parnell? [*Rises.*] Where is he?

MURPHY. He and young Mr. Harrison are in the inner room.

DAVITT. Anyone else?

MURPHY. No, Sir. They just came a few moments ago. I'm to let 'em know when the rest are come.

DAVITT. How did he look?

MURPHY. Haven't you seen him—since—the divorce?

DAVITT. No.

MURPHY. Bad. [*Sits.*] Like a fire burnin' him—inside.

DAVITT. Hell fire.

MURPHY. Look here Mr. Davitt, he's not the first man to be led astray by a woman—nor yet the last.

DAVITT. Him! Of all men I'd a'said—not him.

MURPHY. If I had my way it would be that dirty, sneakin' little spy, with his monocle and his fine talk—

DAVITT. He had a right to sue for divorce. He was in his rights.

MURPHY. He wasn't weepin' about his rights when we ran him for Galway. Not O'Shea.

DAVITT. [*Obstinately.*] Rights is rights.

MURPHY. An' feelin's is feelin's.

DAVITT. [*Savagely.*] Whose feelin's?

MURPHY. [*With a jerk of the head toward the inner room.*] His feelin's—and hers. [*Pleasantly.*] Ever see her?

DAVITT. I have. Hell take her.

MURPHY. Don't, Mr. Davitt.

DAVITT. [*Rises.*] I'll not be the only one, Murphy, before this business is out. [*Knock on the door.*] I don't want to see 'em till I have to. [*Crosses to Down Left door.*]

MURPHY. I'll call ye, Mr. Davitt.

[DAVITT *goes into the small clerk's room.* MURPHY *crosses and opens the door. It is* KATIE.]

KATIE. Mr. Murphy—

MURPHY. [*Perturbed.*] Good evenin'.

KATIE. Mr. Murphy, are Mr. Parnell and Mr. Harrison here?

MURPHY. Yes. They're both here. Shall I tell Mr. Parnell?

KATIE. No—I want to see Monty Harrison. You needn't say who it is. As quickly as possible, please.

MURPHY. [KATIE *steps into the room and* MURPHY *closes the door.*] I'll call him.

KATIE. Don't mention my name, please.

[MURPHY *walks to the door of the inner room and knocks.* MONTY *opens it.*]

MURPHY. Mr. Harrison, will you step here a moment, please.

MONTY. [*Glances back to assure himself that he is not wanted by* PARNELL, *comes into the room closing the door behind him. He is much surprised to see* KATIE.] Mrs. O'Shea!

KATIE. Monty—I'm mad to come here—I know—

MONTY. Shall I tell Mr. Parnell?

KATIE. No. Is Mr. Healy back?

MONTY. Not yet. We'd better talk somewhere else—the Party's meeting.

KATIE. Yes—they didn't want to let me up. But I have a special pass, you know.

MURPHY. Shall I leave you alone?

KATIE. No—please. I'll only be a moment. I saw Mr. Gladstone. I begged him—almost on my knees. I think it's hopeless. But, oh, Monty, even if Gladstone refuses —surely the Party will stand by him— [*He shakes head.*] you don't think the Party— [*He nods. She looks into* MONTY'S *face and reads doubt and sorrow.*] Then— there is only one thing now—they must know why he would not defend himself.

MONTY. [*Alarmed.*] You know Mr. Parnell would not allow it.

KATIE. Oh, Monty, we are long past obeying and disobeying.

MONTY. [*Definite.*] I couldn't—against his orders— and besides— It wouldn't do any good

KATIE. [*Turns to* MURPHY.] Mr. Murphy, Mr. Parnell refused to save himself by defending my husband's suit against him. If he had let the truth come out there would have been no divorce. I would still be Captain O'Shea's wife. Can't they understand? He wouldn't save himself at that price. Can't they be made to understand? Mr. Murphy—don't let them turn against him.

MURPHY. Mrs. O'Shea—there's nothin' I wouldn't do for him.

KATIE. Thank you. [*She smiles up at him and turns to go.*]

MONTY. [*Crosses to her.*] You must go. I'll take you down.

KATIE. No. You may be needed here. I'll go.

MONTY. [*Follows her to door.*] Please let me.

KATIE. No—I'll take the little stair. I won't be seen. That wouldn't help things much, would it? [*She is at the door and smiles up at* MONTY *rather a heart-breaking smile.*] Monty—what are they going to do to him?

MONTY. Don't. Everything will come out all right—I be-lieve—

KATIE. I shall be waiting—at Eltham.

MONTY. It may be terribly late.

KATIE. I shall be waiting. [*She goes out.*]

MONTY. [*Turning his head to avoid letting* MURPHY

see the tears in his eyes.] Mr. Murphy, I must ask you
never to repeat what Mrs. O'Shea has just told you.

MURPHY. Very well, Mr. Harrison.

[*There is a loud knock on the door.* MURPHY *crosses to
it.* MONTY *goes into the inner room again and closes the
door.*]

O'GORMAN. [*Coming in as* MURPHY *opens the door.*]
Good evenin' to ye.

[DAVITT *comes in from the clerk's room.*]

MURPHY. Good evenin', Sir. Were ye expected?

O'GORMAN. That I can't answer, me lad—but I'm here.

MURPHY. [*Dubiously to* DAVITT.] Is it all right?

DAVITT. Let him stay.

O'GORMAN. And why not? There's to be a meetin' of
Irish leaders. Where Ireland is—there am I.

MURPHY. Or where Captain O'Shea is—I'm thinkin'
ye're there too.

O'GORMAN. Captain O'Shea is my very dear and much
injured friend.

MURPHY. A much injured friend—

DAVITT. Let be I tell ye, Murphy. [MURPHY *turns his
back and walks to the window. There is another knock.*]
Come in.

[*Four or five men come in. We will call them* FIRST, SEC-

OND, THIRD, *etc.* "LEADERS." *They say* "Good evening," "How d' you do," "Good evenin' Davitt," *etc.* DAVITT *bows but says nothing. The atmosphere is funereal and no one knows how to lighten it.*]

FIRST LEADER. Good evening. Good evening. It's a bad night.

DAVITT. High wind.

O'GORMAN. [*To* O'KEEFE. *Reminiscently.*] Aye—talkin' o' wind—when I was a lad—about the year—

THIRD LEADER. [*Interrupting.*] Mr. Parnell come yet?

O'GORMAN. [*Peevish at the interruption.*] Mr. Parnell? Are ye really expectin' him this evenin'? I'm thinkin' ye'll have a long wait.

MURPHY. An' what makes ye think that?

O'GORMAN. A man who would stoop—

DAVITT. That'll do!

O'GORMAN. Very well, Mr. Davitt—but I'm sayin' nothin' but what the world's ringin' with. Defend him if ye like—but when he turns tail—

MURPHY. He's never turned his back yet—on friend or foe.

FOURTH LEADER. He will be here tonight?

MURPHY. He *is* here.

[*The door opens and* HEALY *and* JOHN REDMOND *come*

in. HEALY *is flushed and excited.* REDMOND *quiet and set.*]

HEALY. Well—boys— [*He looks around.*] Where's Mr. Parnell?

MURPHY. In there. I'm to tell him when you've come.

HEALY. Thank you.

[*Silence falls on the room. They look at each other anxiously and then at the door to the inner room.* DAVITT *is staring at the floor.* MURPHY *crosses and knocks at the door.* MONTY *opens it.*]

MURPHY. Will ye tell Mr. Parnell we're waitin' for him?

MONTY. [*Looks around and sees that* HEALY *and* REDMOND *are come.*] Very well.

[*He turns back into the room.* PARNELL *comes to the door deadly white, only his dark eyes burning curiously. He comes in with that quiet, aloof and quite unconscious dignity which was his to so singular a degree.*]

PARNELL. Good evening, gentlemen. [*He looks at* HEALY *and* REDMOND *then his glance pauses for a moment on* MICHAEL DAVITT. DAVITT *drops his eyes.*] Will you be seated? [REDMOND *indicates the large chair at the back of the table.* PARNELL *takes it.*] Mr. Healy, did you and Mr. Redmond succeed in getting an interview with Mr. Gladstone?

HEALY. We did.

PARNELL. In that case we are ready for discussion.

O'GORMAN. Discussion of what?

PARNELL. [*As though there had been no remark.*] This is in no sense a formal meeting but a gathering of leaders to talk over our future policy.

SECOND LEADER. In regard to what?

PARNELL. In regard to the steps we must take to insure a safe majority for the Home Rule Bill.

O'GORMAN. I'm of the opinion there's other matters to come up before that.

PARNELL. The remark is out of order.

O'GORMAN. I protest. [*He looks around for encouragement but gets none. There are remarks of* "Right of the chair," "Out of order."]

PARNELL. Sixteen years ago I conceived the idea of an Irish Party welded into one complete whole. All the different factions of Ireland fighting together for one purpose, the freedom of Ireland. Our Party oath "Sit together, act together, vote together." [*Cries of* "aye," "That we have" *etc.*] I knew that only by presenting a common front to the enemy could we hope for victory. Ten years ago I was elected leader of that Party. [*There is dead silence.*] You have given me absolute loyalty, absolute obedience, and we have at last forced on the English the necessity of granting Home Rule to Ireland. ["Hear." "Hear."] By our votes the Liberals have been swept to power. In return Mr. Gladstone promised us Home Rule. He was to move the first reading of the

Bill this session. Now, for personal reasons, which I shall not discuss here—

SECOND LEADER. [*Interrupting.*] That's what we've come for.

O'GORMAN. What are Mr. Gladstone's objections?

["Aye," "What's the matter with Gladstone," "Personal reasons" *etc.*]

PARNELL. Mr. Gladstone refuses to continue his support because he objects to me, personally as Leader of the Irish Party.

REDMOND. Since when have we taken orders from an Englishman?

[*The* FOURTH LEADER *rises to his feet. He is friendly to* PARNELL *but sorely troubled as to the wisest course.* PARNELL *looks at them and quiets by the sheer force of his personality the remarks which have followed* REDMOND'S *question.*]

FOURTH LEADER. Mr. Parnell, if you, as Leader of the Irish Party are the stumbling block to Home Rule, if because of you a Parliament for Ireland is endangered, then, for the sake of the Party, for the sake of Ireland— I think you should resign.

["Hear," Hear," "That's what I say"]

PARNELL. [*Very quietly.*] I am in entire agreement with you.

[DAVITT'S *head comes up. He looks at* PARNELL.]

FOURTH LEADER. Well—Mr. Parnell—all I can say is— if we are in agreement—there is no need for further discussion.

HEALY. [*Jumps to his feet and with much emotion.*] Mr. Parnell, I believe you have chosen the course of wisdom, for Ireland and for yourself. If at some future time you elect to return and again lead your people I shall be among the first to welcome you as Chief. [*He sits down.*]

PARNELL. [*He rises slowly to his feet. He has that queer calmness of manner, that strange aloofness which made him so irresistible to the Irish people.*] In a public letter Mr. Gladstone demands my resignation. Putting aside the question of what right he, or any other Englishman, has to dictate to us, I say, putting this aside, although I consider it fundamental, I have replied to Mr. Gladstone. Since I am no longer acceptable to him as Leader of the Irish Party, I have told him I will resign at once [*There is a complete hush over the room.*] —if he will give me his assurance—

DAVITT. [*Interrupting.*] In writing.

MURPHY. Aye—an' then put it in a glass case.

PARNELL. [*As though there had been no interruption.*] I said I would resign if he would give me his word that he would continue to support the Home Rule Bill. [LEADERS: "Aye."] Gentlemen, Mr. Healy and Mr. Redmond have just left Mr. Gladstone. I have not talked to them. Mr. Healy, will you tell us the result of your visit.

[*The hush still holds.* HEALY *rises to his feet. He is somewhat ill at ease and prepared to be combative.*]

HEALY. Yes, Mr. Gladstone assured us of his heartfelt desire that Ireland should have Home Rule—

MURPHY. Will he vote for it?

HEALY. He received us with the greatest courtesy and politeness—

DAVITT. An' what did he promise ye?

HEALY. [*Stung.*] Am I to be interrupted in this manner?

PARNELL. Come to the point, Mr. Healy. Did he, or did he not promise to support Home Rule?

REDMOND. [*Quietly, but in a very clear voice.*] He did not.

[*Reaction.*]

HEALY. [*To all—not* PARNELL.] He did not—and I don't think he could be expected to. He told us—and I agree with him—that our first business was to choose a Leader. Then he would discuss the question of Home Rule.

MURPHY. He ran all around ye—that's the size of it.

HEALY. As long as the world can point a finger of shame at the man who represents Ireland, what favors can ye expect?

DAVITT. Favors—since when has Ireland asked favors? It's rights we're askin' an' it's rights we'll get.

KELLY. Who'll get them for you? Who forced the English to consider Home Rule? Who is the one man among us who can force them? Do you expect them to hand it to you on a platter? Who'll get you your rights?

HEALY. Is Mr. Parnell the only man who can face Gladstone?

MURPHY. That was a foine fight ye put up tonight, Tim Healy.

REDMOND. Why is Mr. Gladstone so anxious to rid us of our Leader? Why does he wrap around him the mantle of righteousness and demand a sacrifice? Because the one man who can give him orders, the one man who can give orders to the House of Commons—to England— is Charles Stewart Parnell. Will you sell him to keep the favor of the English? Then I ask what will you get in return?

HEALY. [*Shouting.*] *Home Rule!* That's what we'll get.

PARNELL. Gentlemen— [*They sit.* PARNELL *rises.*] You really think that? You really think that Mr. Gladstone is burning with a desire to free Ireland? I wish I could be so trustful. Gentlemen, remember you are dealing with an unrivaled sophist—a man from whom it is as impossible to get a direct answer to a simple question, as it is impossible for me to give an indirect one. We gave him our votes—we have carried out our part—now—

HEALY. [*Shouting—loudly.*] And what's put him off? What's broken the alliance?

REDMOND. Mr. Gladstone has broken it?

HEALY. No—it perished in the stench of a divorce court.

[*Bedlam. Cries of* "Shame," "Hear," "Away with him" *etc.* REDMOND *and* MONTY *spring to* PARNELL'S *side. He stands staring at* HEALY, *deadly pale and very quiet.*]

O'GORMAN. [*Above the din.*] And not a word in his own defense.

MURPHY. It's not the first time in history a man has not opened his mouth.

PARNELL. [*Raises his hand. There is almost instant silence.*] I do not intend to plead to your excuses or reasons. I am—as I am. But I do claim that never in thought, word, or deed have I been false to Ireland. I ask you tonight, not to be swayed by Mr. Gladstone's sudden resort to pious scruple, nor by any personal hate or loyalty you may feel for me. Your duty is clear— ["Aye," "That it is," *etc.*] Ireland's welfare should be your sole consideration.

DAVITT. Aye—it is.

PARNELL. If you think you can fight Gladstone without me, that is for you to decide, but—don't sell me for nothing. If you surrender me—if you throw me to him —it is your bounden duty to secure value for the sacrifice. [*He pauses and looks at them.*] I have a Parliament in the hollow of my hand. I give you my word I will get it for you—if you will let me.

REDMOND. [*Rises. Patriotic fervor.*] Gentlemen— Charles Parnell is not only the leader—he is the *Master* of the Irish Party—

HEALY. And who is the *Mistress*?

[PARNELL *hurls himself at* HEALY *but* MONTY *and* DA-VITT *hold him back.*]

PARNELL. When a lying Irishman dares insult a woman in the presence of Irishmen—

[*Cries of* "Shame, Shame, Shame!"]

REDMOND. Gentlemen, the time has come to stop this discussion.

THIRD LEADER. Put the motion.

O'GORMAN. VOTE.

KELLY. VOTE.

TREXLER. VOTE.

HEALY. [*Rises. To the men.*] You'll have no vote from me this night. Do you think Parnell can get Home Rule? He'll get you nothing but insults. What can you expect if ye are lead by a man whose name is a stench in the nostrils of decent people. Will you besmirch Ireland by such a Leadership? Then I'm done with you. The Irish people shall know the issues in this matter—an' I'll not shirk the tellin'—

PARNELL. Go to the people, Tim Healy—as I shall do. I appeal to the people of Ireland. They've never failed me yet. On their answer I stand or fall.

HEALY. I take the challenge. From tonight there's a new Irish Party. Those who are with me— [O'GORMAN *rises.*] those who have the honour of Ireland at heart—

[TREXLER *rises.*] who would have a new Party—and a new leader—follow me. I bid you good evening.

[HEALY *exits followed by* O'GORMAN, TREXLER, O'KEEFE *and* KELLY *who rises after* TREXLER *exits.*]

[DAVITT *is sitting staring at floor. Suddenly he realizes that* HEALY *and his crowd are gone.* REDMOND, MURPHY *and* MONTY *are looking at* PARNELL *but* PARNELL *is looking at* DAVITT. *One of* PARNELL'S *rare smiles come to his lips.* DAVITT *looks at him with eyes of utter woe. Then slowly he raises himself and starts toward the door without looking back.* PARNELL'S *face again becomes the cold mask he usually shows his followers. As* DAVITT *reaches the door* PARNELL *sways and puts his hand to his side.* REDMOND *and* MONTY *catch him and lower him into the chair. At the sound of feet* DAVITT *turns.*]

DAVITT. What is it? Are ye hurt?

PARNELL. Monty! [MONTY *gets from* PARNELL'S *vest pocket a small capsule of amyl nitrate. He breaks it on a handkerchief and holds it to* PARNELL. *In a few moments the pain is lessened.*] That's better. I'm quite all right.

REDMOND. We will help you to your hotel.

PARNELL. [*Still not breathing with ease.*] No. I'm going—home. [DAVITT *and* MURPHY *look at each other.*] Monty—

MONTY. Yes, Sir.

PARNELL. Take a cab—drive ahead—. Tell her—it's nothing—I'm quite all right.

MONTY. Mr. Parnell—oughtn't you to rest first? It's a long drive to Eltham.

[PARNELL *raises his head and makes an effort to speak but no words come.*]

DAVITT. [*Fiercely.*] Ye'll take him where he wants to be. [*He looks at* MONTY *who goes on out.*] Murphy— see that Mr. Parnell's carriage is waitin'.

[MURPHY *follows* MONTY *out the door.* REDMOND *starts to help* PARNELL.]

PARNELL. [*Rising slowly from the chair.*] I shall be quite all right now. [REDMOND *takes his arm and together they start for the door.* DAVITT *crosses ahead and opens it. As* PARNELL *reaches the door looks at* DAVITT *standing waiting for him to pass through.*] Thank you —Michael.

[*The curtain falls as they go out,* DAVITT *following.*]

CURTAIN

ACT THREE

Scene III

SCENE—*The drawing room at Eltham.*
Late evening.
The fire has burned low. One lamp sheds a
pool of light near the fireplace. A moaning
wind hurls itself against the window.
KATIE *enters from study—looks out Left*
window—Crosses to fire—fixes logs—stands
facing it.
The door opens and PHYLLIS *comes in with a*
small tray of tea.

PHYLLIS. [*Crosses to a table and puts down the tray.*]
Won't ye be afther havin' a bit o' hot tay, Ma'am?

KATIE. [*Without turning.*] Phyllis,—that wind.

PHYLLIS. [*Crosses Down with tea.*] Sure a bit o' tay is
what ye need.

KATIE. No thank you.

PHYLLIS. Excuse me spakin', Ma'am—but ye look so
white—shure a bit o' tay.

KATIE. I'm sorry, Phyllis. I can't. [*Crosses to the table.*
PHYLLIS *returns tea to table.*] You must have made it
for me yourself, Phyllis.

PHYLLIS. [*Handing* KATIE *a cup.*] Cook's been in bed these two hours.

KATIE. [*Takes the cup.*] Thank you, Phyllis. Listen— [*Puts the cup down hastily.*] Did you hear wheels?

PHYLLIS. [*At Upper Right window.*] Sure ye could hear nothin' over this wind.

KATIE. Look.

PHYLLIS. [*Crosses to the window.*] It's so dark ye can't see anything but your own face in the window pane.

[MONTY *appears at the door.*]

MONTY. Mrs. O'Shea.

KATIE. Monty—where is he?

MONTY. I took a cab ahead. Mr. Parnell told me to tell you that he was quite all right.

KATIE. Quite all right— Is he ill?

MONTY. A little. Not a bad attack.

KATIE. Was it because of the meeting? What did they do? Listen, he's here. Monty you let him in. [MONTY *crosses to her.*] Phyllis, go into the study and bring the brandy. [*She exits.*]

[PHYLLIS *has opened the front door and voices are heard.* "Which way?" "This way, please, Sir." PARNELL *appears at the door leaning on* MURPHY'S *arm.* DAVITT *is just behind him. They pause for a second and* PARNELL *looks at* KATIE. *She goes to him. He leaves* MURPHY *and puts his arm about her. It is an embrace as well as a confession of his need for support.* KATIE *looks into his eyes and he smiles.*]

KATIE. Come to the fire. [*They move together to the fire.* MONTY *springs forward to help lower* PARNELL *into the chair.* KATIE *removes muffler, hands it to* MONTY —*he gives it to* PHYLLIS. KATIE *crosses to slippers—returns—takes off shoes.* DAVITT *and* MURPHY *stand watching, ill at ease and miserably anxious.*]

PARNELL. There— [*He sits.*] That's better. Thank you.

MONTY. You'll be all right now.

MURPHY. Sure—he'll be foine.

PARNELL. Yes. I'm very grateful to you for coming down with me. Thank you. [*To* MONTY.] Monty—take them into the study and see that they have something to drink.

[*Men cross to door.* PHYLLIS *exits with coat and shoes.*]

DAVITT. I'll not be drinkin', thank you.

PARNELL. [*Looking straight at* DAVITT.] Yes, Michael. [*With a smile.*] On me.

DAVITT. Thank you.

MONTY. [*Starting to the door.*] If you'll come with me, gentlemen—

MURPHY. [*Leaving.*] A drop or two'll not come amiss this night.

KATIE. Will you have some brandy?

PARNELL. No— [KATIE *bows her head but says nothing. The* THREE MEN *go out, closing the door after them.* KATIE *drops on her knees by* PARNELL'S *chair.* PARNELL'S *first words are said with some difficulty but gradually his strength, flares up. Takes her hands.*] Well— Katie—the Old Spider has got nearly all my flies in his web. Healy—

KATIE. Oh, *no*—

PARNELL. And Michael—

KATIE. Michael! Michael Davitt!

PARNELL. Michael's gone too.

KATIE. Fools!

PARNELL. Children! We shall have to fight, Katie. Can you bear it?

KATIE. If you can. Oh, I tried—I begged him—

PARNELL. My darling— I never really thought for an instant the Old Spider—

KATIE. He's not a spider, he's a politician and a devout Churchman.

PARNELL. But he's not done with me—not yet. I'll fight him.

KATIE. But, darling, not now—you must rest now.

PARNELL. I shall go to the people.

KATIE. Yes, dear—yes—later on—

PARNELL. I shall write a letter to the people of Ireland.

KATIE. But you are ill. You must let—some of the others write it for you.

PARNELL. [*With a smile.*] No. I refuse to go down to posterity talking bad English. I shall fight—if he thinks I'm beaten—

KATIE. Of course you're not. But first you're going to come away with me—now.

PARNELL. [*Dreamily.*] Where there is sun.

KATIE. [*Eagerly.*] Algiers—

PARNELL. [*Still quiet.*] Or Carcasonne. Yes, Katie—when this fight is over—

KATIE. Now—now—you must come now. We will forget, darling—forget everything.

PARNELL. Forget—that I ran away?

KATIE. After a while you will come back—then—

PARNELL. [*Comes forward.*] Katie—don't make me less than the man you loved. I'll fight— [*He has a sudden spasm of pain.* KATIE *alarmed starts to get up to go for help. But he recovers quickly.*] Don't go. Don't leave me.

KATIE. [*Sits.*] I was going to get help.

PARNELL. There is nothing to do. You know that. Don't leave me. Give me your hand. [KATIE *puts her hand in his.*] Don't ever leave me. [PARNELL *seems to doze for a moment. Then he starts up, releasing* KATIE'S *hand. Wildly.*] I have a Parliament for you. Kill me and you kill Ireland. [*He realizes that he has been talking wildly.*] I was dreaming.

KATIE. Try to rest a little, dear.

PARNELL. Yes. [*He leans back and closes his eyes. Then he starts up again. Sadly to self.*] Michael— Michael—

KATIE. Yes, dear, yes. Won't you rest now?

PARNELL. Where is your hand. Don't leave me.

[KATIE *puts her hand in his.*]

KATIE. I won't leave you.

PARNELL. Kiss me. [*She leans forward and kisses him on the mouth. He dies in her arms.*]

KATIE. [*Looks at him closely.*] Darling—darling, speak to me. [*She leans against him. Her hands against his shoulders almost as though she would shake him.*] No— speak to me—No—No—I won't leave you—I'm here. Speak to me. [*There is only silence.*] Oh, God— Oh, God—dear God— [*She gathers his head to her shoulder almost as though she had a child in her arms, swaying a little. Then she rises slowly and crosses to the door, flings it open.*] Monty!— [*Turns.*] *Monty!*

[*The* THREE MEN *rush into the room,* MONTY *first. He looks at* KATIE *then at the figure in the chair. He crosses,*

DAVITT *and* MURPHY *following him.* MONTY *picks up the lifeless hand and then lays it quietly down. He looks at the other two. They cross themselves and* DAVITT *drops on his knees by the chair and begins to murmur a prayer for the dead.*]

DAVITT. [*In a sort of amazement.*] He's gone. [*Falls on his knees. To* PARNELL.] I was only thinkin' of Ireland.

KATIE. Monty—he will miss me so.

MONTY. [*At* PARNELL— *Loyal but ever literal.*] You mean—you will miss him.

KATIE. [*With agony in her voice.*] Oh, Monty—*is* that all I mean?

MONTY. [*To her.*] Won't you come away?

KATIE. [*Unemotionally.*] I killed him.

[DAVITT *hears her. He rises to his feet, crossing himself.*]

DAVITT. [*Going to* KATIE.] No. No more than all of us. [*Slowly.*] Some things—*have* to happen.

CURTAIN